WOODWORKING WITH
POWER TOOLS

TOOLS, TECHNIQUES & PROJECTS

T0317112

EDITORS OF **FINE WOODWORKING**

The Taunton Press

THE TAUNTON PRESS, INC.
63 South Main Street
Newtown, CT 06470-2344
E-mail: tp@taunton.com

EDITORS: Peter Chapman, Christina Glennon
COPY EDITOR: Carolyn Mandarano
INDEXER: Jim Curtis
JACKET/COVER DESIGN: Guido Caroti
INTERIOR DESIGN: Carol Singer
LAYOUT: Barbara Cottingham, Lynne Phillips

Fine Woodworking® is a trademark of The Taunton Press, Inc., registered in the U.S. Patent and
Trademark Office.

The following names/manufacturers appearing in *Woodworking with Power Tools* are
trademarks: Amana® Tool, Central Machinery®, Delta®, DeWalt®, Dominoes®, Dust Right®,
Freud®, General® International, General® Tools, Gorilla®, Grizzly®, JET®, Merle®,
Osmo Polyx®-Oil, Porter-Cable®, Powermatic®, Ridgid®, Rikon®, Shop Fox®, SuperCut™
WoodSaver Plus, Titebond®

Library of Congress Cataloging-in-Publication Data

Title: Woodworking with power tools : tools, techniques & projects / editors
  of Fine woodworking.
Other titles: Fine woodworking.
Description: Newtown, CT : The Taunton Press, Inc., [2019] | Includes index.
Identifiers: LCCN 2018039810 | ISBN 9781641550109
Subjects: LCSH: Woodwork--Equipment and supplies. | Power tools.
Classification: LCC TT153.5 .W646 2019 | DDC 684/.083--dc23
LC record available at https://lccn.loc.gov/2018039810

Printed in the United States of America
10 9 8 7 6 5 4 3 2 1

ABOUT YOUR SAFETY: Working wood is inherently dangerous. Using hand
or power tools improperly or ignoring safety practices can lead to permanent injury
or even death. Don't try to perform operations you learn about here (or elsewhere)
unless you're certain they are safe for you. If something about an operation doesn't
feel right, don't do it. Look for another way. We want you to enjoy the craft, so please
keep safety foremost in your mind whenever you're in the shop.

ACKNOWLEDGMENTS

Special thanks to the authors, editors, art directors, copy editors, and other staff members of *Fine Woodworking* who contributed to the development of the chapters in this book.

Contents

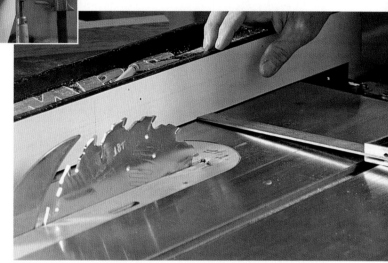

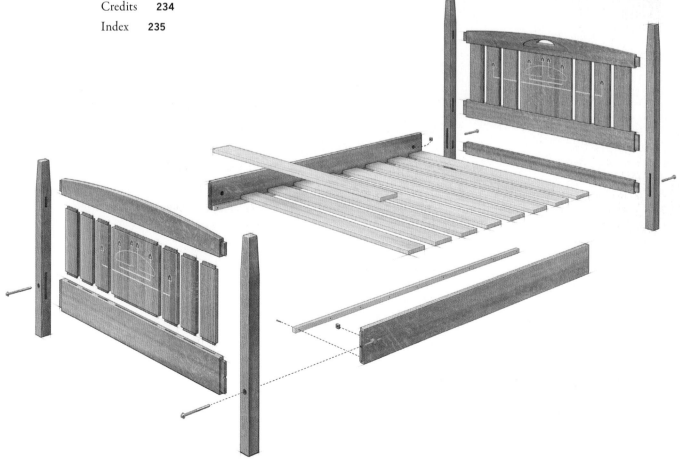

Introduction

Hand-tool woodworking has been on the upswing in recent years. There are classes, books, and projects based on pre-industrial woodworking popping up all over. Walk into the woods on a weekend and you may stumble across a circle of spoon carvers wielding hewing axes and sloyd knives. Yet for nearly all woodworkers, even those attracted to hand-tool work as well, machines and powered hand tools remain at the center of the craft.

In terms of the fundamental jobs they perform, the principal machines in a typical woodshop—tablesaw, bandsaw, drill press, jointer, and planer—haven't changed that much in the century and a half or so since they were invented. But upgrades in the way they perform those tasks seem to occur weekly, and the flow of innovations people make in the way they use their machines is unending.

This book, which collects articles first published in *Fine Woodworking* magazine, will bring you up to date on which new machines are best; which blades, bits, and accessories to consider acquiring; and what clever new techniques makers have devised. In addition to stationary machines, the book covers routers, track saws, and dust collection. And it also presents a bevy of excellent projects tailored to machine work, from stunning boxes made on the bandsaw to a handsome trestle table with tablesawn joinery and a bookcase whose building blends hand- and power-tool processes.

Ladies and gentlemen, start your engines.

—Jonathan Binzen, Deputy Editor
Fine Woodworking

PART ONE

TOOLS

Cabinet Saws for the Home Shop

ROLAND JOHNSON

It would be nice to have a full-size cabinet saw in your home shop. But there are roadblocks to purchasing one. Because the machine can cost more than $3,000, it can be difficult to fit one in your tool budget. A cabinet saw also requires a 240-volt circuit, which many of us don't have in our garage and basement shops. Finally, it can take up a lot of space.

Not too long ago, the only alternative to a full-size cabinet saw was a contractor saw, but it is fussy to adjust, has poor dust collection, and can be underpowered for furniture making. Now there's a new style of saw that will fit the bill for most home shops: a compact saw that gives you all of the benefits of a cabinet saw—power, good dust collection, vibration-dampening mass, and

No problem with runout. Johnson checked every saw for runout at the arbor flange (where it really matters) and found that none of the saws had any.

Parallelism at 45° and 90° was impressive, too. With the blade at each angle, most of the saws were close enough to parallel that cuts were not affected.

Plenty of muscle for furniture making. None of the saws had trouble ripping 8/4 hard maple, and all have enough power to cut just about anything you'd need to make furniture.

Safety features that are easy to use. The biggest recent improvement in tablesaws is the quality and convenience of the riving knife and blade guards that come with them. All of the saws have good knives and guards.

easy adjustments—for less money. And it all can run on a 110-volt circuit.

Fine Woodworking asked me to compare compact saws head to head. I checked them for accuracy, including arbor flange runout, and whether the blade was parallel to the miter slot. I also looked at the sturdiness and accuracy of the rip fence, the saw's ability to hold settings for tilt and elevation, power switch placement, and the ease of changing blades. To gauge their power, I ripped 8/4 hard maple and timed each rip. I repeated the process numerous times for each saw, using both a standard-kerf and a thin-kerf blade.

After the tests, it was clear that the SawStop PCS175 was the Best Overall. It was dead accurate, has a top-quality fit and finish, is the most user-friendly saw, and has SawStop's flesh-sensing technology and blade brake. The Best Value among the saws is the Grizzly G0715P. It's heavy, accurate, has good power, and costs just $825.

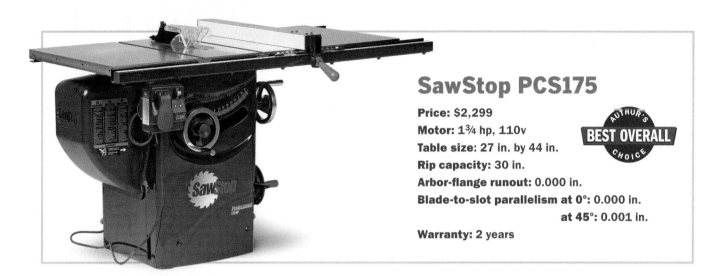

SawStop PCS175

Price: $2,299
Motor: 1¾ hp, 110v
Table size: 27 in. by 44 in.
Rip capacity: 30 in.
Arbor-flange runout: 0.000 in.
Blade-to-slot parallelism at 0°: 0.000 in.
                              at 45°: 0.001 in.

Warranty: 2 years

AUTHOR'S CHOICE **BEST OVERALL**

SawStop PCS175

Even without its well-known blade brake, the SawStop is a great saw. It has very good ripping power. The dust collection was good, especially considering that the blade is enclosed only on one side to make room for the blade-brake cartridge. A 4-in. hose connects the blade shroud to a port in the cabinet. Everything else about the PCS175 is smooth. The fence locked tightly and glided like skates on ice, at least in part due to two small wheels on the underside of the fence at the end opposite the handle. You can move the fence with one finger. The tilt and elevation wheels had no backlash and turned beautifully.

Switching from the riving knife to the blade guard took no time at all. And the guard is very good. There are three independent, but connected, leaves on each side of the blade. Their light weight made it easy to push thin or light stock under the guard, and the leaves fall sequentially back into position. There is no locking device for holding the leaves off the table, but it was easy to lift the leaves manually above the fence for ripping narrow stock. When making a replacement insert plate, you have to do some extra work to make way for the safety gear, a small inconvenience that doesn't outweigh the safety aspect. Overall, the SawStop PCS175 is excellent. Throw in its safety device, and it's tremendous.

Quick exchange from riving knife to guard. A big, easy-to-reach lever is all you need to free them on the SawStop.

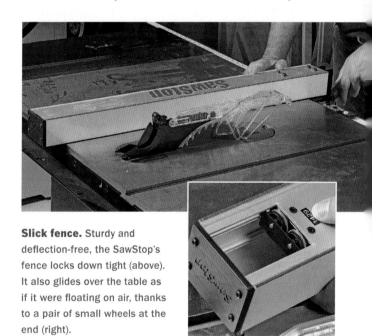

Slick fence. Sturdy and deflection-free, the SawStop's fence locks down tight (above). It also glides over the table as if it were floating on air, thanks to a pair of small wheels at the end (right).

Baileigh TS-1044H

Price: $1,595
Motor: 1¾ hp, 110v
Table size: 27 in. by 44 in.
Rip capacity: 36 in.
Arbor-flange runout: 0.000 in.
Blade-to-slot parallelism at 0°: 0.006 in.
at 45°: 0.026 in.

Warranty: 1 year

Baileigh TS-1044H

Cabinet saws are heavy and difficult to move by yourself, which is something you might need to do in a home shop that doubles as a garage. Baileigh addressed the problem by mounting four wheels inside the TS-1044H's cabinet. They allow you to roll the saw forward and back, but not side to side. To make turns, you can lift up on the fence rails and rotate the saw. When you don't need the mobility, the wheels lock with thumbscrews.

The saw's fence is T-square style and worked very well. It's the only fence in the test that comes with a digital readout that displays the distance between the fence and blade down to thousandths of an inch. It's easy to zero out when you change blades, and I found it to be accurate. Dust collection was fair.

The Baileigh did very well in the ripping test, but its miter slot was significantly out of parallel to the blade with the blade tilted to 45°. Fortunately, the trunnions are mounted to the cabinet, which makes it easy to fix. The power switch is very low on the cabinet, making it hard to reach with your hand or knee. Also, the riving knife and blade guard lock in place with the spin of a star knob. It's not difficult, but it is less convenient than the locking mechanisms on the Grizzly, SawStop, and Powermatic saws.

Digital fence readout. The distance from the blade to the fence is displayed to a thousandth of an inch, and it's accurate.

Built-in mobile base. Four wheels in the cabinet allow you to move the saw forward and back. The wheels lock with a few turns of a thumbwheel.

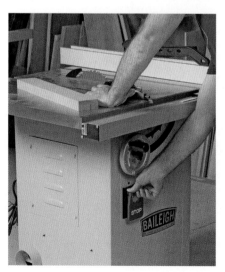

Long reach for the power switch. Located beneath the height adjustment wheel, the switch requires you to lean over too far.

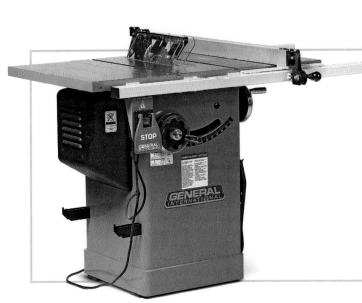

General Intl. 50-200R M1

Price: $1,200
Motor: 2 hp, 230v
Table size: 20³⁄₁₆ in. by 44³⁄₁₆ in.
Rip capacity: 30 in.
Arbor-flange runout: 0.000 in.
Blade-to-slot parallelism at 0°: 0.001 in.
                        at 45°: 0.012 in.
Warranty: Limited lifetime

General Intl. 50-200R M1

There's a 2-hp motor inside the cabinet of the 50-200R M1, and it powered the saw through the ripping test better than any of the other saws. It comes wired for 230 volts, but can be rewired for 115. Another highlight of the saw was how easy it was to switch between the riving knife and blade guard. Just flip a lever and pull up. Unfortunately, when the lever is in the locked position you cannot take a blade off the arbor, so you have to flip the lever up whenever you change blades. The arbor lock also made blade changes difficult because it requires you to push a small pin into a hole in the arbor. The pin barely fits

into the hole, and depressing the plunger for the pin wasn't easy.

Large handwheels made adjusting the height and tilt of the blade smooth and easy. The power switch is mounted to the front fence rail and made it a breeze to turn the saw on and off. The off paddle is so big that you can easily push it in with your thigh, a good thing when you need both hands to hold a workpiece steady on the table. Dust collection was good, too. There's a 4-in. port on the outside of the cabinet. It splits inside, with a 2-in. hose running up to the blade shroud and the other half open to suck in anything that falls to the cabinet bottom.

Big wheels and paddle switch. Adjusting the blade's height and tilt was quick and effortless on the General, and there was plenty of clearance for your hand as you spun the wheel. The stop paddle is big and easy to find with your hand or leg.

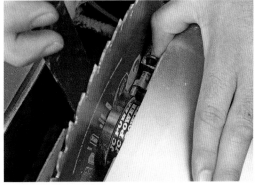

Tricky arbor lock. Located between the blade and throat opening—a tight squeeze for most hands—it took a fair amount of force to press the locking pin into a hole in the arbor.

Powermatic PM1000

Price: $2,000
Motor: 1¾ hp, 115v
Table size: 27 in. by 40 in.
Rip capacity: 30 in.
Arbor-flange runout: 0.001 in.
Blade-to-slot parallelism at 0°: 0.000 in.
at 45°: 0.002 in.
Warranty: 5 years

Powermatic PM1000

This is an excellent saw. It seems to me like a slightly smaller, but no less impressive, version of the PM2000, a cabinet saw that I've used in my shop for the last decade. The fit and finish were as neat as a pin. Equipped with a 1¾-hp motor, the PM1000 did very well in the ripping test. It's massive, too, weighed down by big cast-iron trunnions and a stout motor and arbor assembly. The T-square-style fence was solid, had the least amount of deflection, and was simply bigger and beefier than the other fences.

The riving knife and blade guard are locked in place by a cam clamp, making switches from one to the other quick and painless. There is a single leaf on each side of the blade guard, and they operate independently, so it's no problem to raise one above the fence for thin rips. A detent holds the leaf up. Blade changes are a breeze, too, thanks to an easy-to-use plunge lock on the arbor. The power switch is another great convenience, as it's perfectly positioned at hip height and easy to find with your hand or hip. Dust collection was good, too.

As good as the PM1000 is, it's a microscopically close second to the SawStop, only because it doesn't have a safety system that's equal to that on the SawStop.

Adjustment wheels roll easily. A few fingers on the knob is all it takes to spin the height and tilt wheels. The action is smooth, with no lash in the gears.

Cam lever simplifies riving knife. The lever is within easy reach and can be opened and closed with just two fingers.

A great arbor lock. There's plenty of room for your thumb, and it takes little effort to depress the lock.

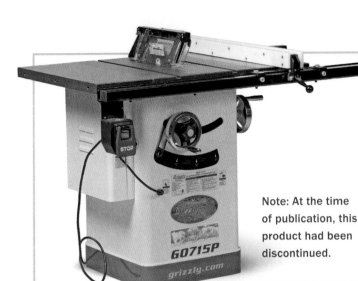

Grizzly G0715P

Price: $825
Motor: 2 hp, 220v
Table size: 27 in. by 40 in.
Rip capacity: 30 in.
Arbor-flange runout: 0.000 in.
Blade-to-slot parallelism at 0°: 0.009 in.
                              at 45°: 0.004 in.

Warranty: 1 year

BEST VALUE — AUTHOR'S CHOICE

Note: At the time of publication, this product had been discontinued.

Grizzly G0715P

With the Grizzly you get a lot of saw for well under $1,000. Powered by a 2-hp motor, the G0715P has plenty of muscle and did very well in the ripping test. (It comes wired for 220 volts, but can be rewired for 110.) The T-square style fence is stout and locked down square with no deflection. Even though there is no blade shroud, dust collection was still quite good, and a big hinged door over the motor makes it easy to vacuum out any dust that falls to the bottom of the cabinet.

The release mechanism for the riving knife and blade guard was easily the most convenient in the test. You don't have to remove the throat plate to switch between the knife and guard. Just slide a thumbwheel back and to the side, and the riving knife is released. Slide in the guard, push the thumbwheel to the side and forward, and it locks the knife into place. Wonderful! The blade guard is good, with a leaf on each side of the blade. The leaves pivot up as wood is fed under them and rise independently so that you can raise just one for thin rips. The arbor lock worked well and was easy to access, making single-wrench blade changes convenient. A minor downside is that the throat plate is very thin, which complicates making a zero-clearance insert for it.

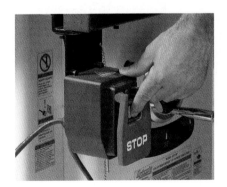

Power switch is hard to miss. The Grizzly's switch is easy to find while you keep your eyes on the blade and workpiece, making for safer transitions at the start and end of a cut.

Awesome riving knife removal. There's no need to remove the throat plate, and all you have to do is move a small thumbwheel to free the knife or guard.

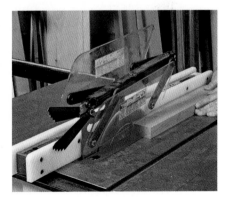

Guard works for thin rips. One side can be rotated up above the fence, while the other side stays down to cover the blade.

Tune Your Tablesaw

ELLEN KASPERN

Most of my projects revolve around a tablesaw. When it's working well, I can make accurate rips, crosscuts, and even coves. All are safe and efficient with a well-tuned saw. But a tablesaw needs regular maintenance; otherwise, using it is at best frustrating and at worst dangerous. If you run through three simple but crucial steps to tune your tablesaw, you'll be back to accurate and safe woodworking in no time.

The goal of the tune-up is to make the blade, table slots, and fence parallel and square. All I need to set my cabinet saw are a reliable 12-in. combination square, a dial indicator, a socket wrench, and some brass shims.

Cleaner Rips, Crosscuts, and Miters

No matter the tablesaw, if it's not tuned properly, it won't be capable of fine woodworking—and worse, it could very well be dangerous. But with just a handful of common tools, you can tune up your saw for all manner of cuts in a couple of hours. Let a North Bennet Street School teacher show you how.

TIP Start flush and square. Before anything, adjust the insert if necessary; it must be flush with the tabletop so the square registers off a good, flat surface. Adjust the blade to 90° and you're ready to begin the tune-up.

Align the top to the blade. With the square's head against the left side of the right slot, slide the ruler until it gently rubs a tooth. Kaspern moves the blade slightly so the tooth rubs the end of the ruler. Lock the ruler here (top). Rotate the blade and register off the same tooth at the back (above). You want the tooth to rub the ruler the same amount as it did at the front. If it doesn't, you need to loosen and rotate the top.

Tap it home. After loosening three of the bolts that attach the top to the cabinet, use the tight bolt as a pivot point to bring the miter slot into parallel with the blade.

Rotate the Top for Parallel

If the distance from the miter slot to the blade is different at the front than at the back, loosen the bolts and tap the top to correct it. Check with the square after each tap and again after you retighten the top.

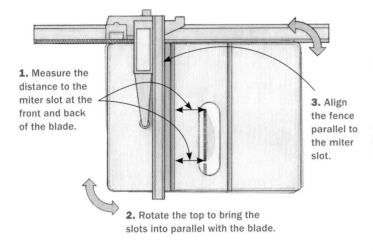

1. Measure the distance to the miter slot at the front and back of the blade.

3. Align the fence parallel to the miter slot.

2. Rotate the top to bring the slots into parallel with the blade.

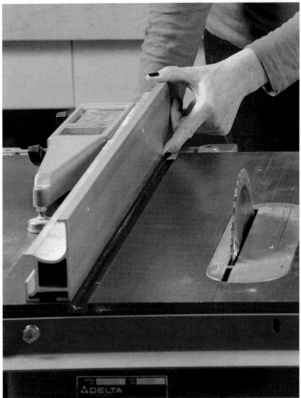

Align the fence to the top. Use your finger to make sure the fence is flush to the miter slot at the front. Then check the back. Be sure the fence doesn't overlap the slot at the back, because if it does, you risk kickback. You can double-check for flush with a straightedge.

Start at the blade and slots

The tune-up starts with the blade at exactly 90°. Raise the blade as high as it will go, set the square against it, and look for any light between the ruler and the blade. If you see some, the blade's not square. Adjust it until it is.

Now that the blade is at 90°, you'll adjust the tabletop so the miter-gauge slots are parallel to the blade. Put the square's head against the left side of the right-hand slot and the ruler at the front of the blade. Carefully slide the ruler out toward the blade until it lightly rubs a tooth. If you're using a rip blade, pick any tooth. If the blade's a crosscut or combination, pick a rip tooth or a tooth angling to the right. Once the ruler slightly touches the tooth, lock the square at that setting.

Move the square and the same tooth to the back. As before, the head of the square should be against the left side of the right slot. If the slot is parallel to the blade, the tooth will touch the ruler the same amount. If the tooth doesn't touch or it rubs too much, you'll have to adjust the table.

On cabinet saws, the tabletop can be adjusted independently of the blade because the two aren't connected. To adjust the tabletop, loosen three of the four bolts that attach the top to the cabinet. The fourth bolt will serve as the pivot point. Tap the top until the miter slot is parallel to the blade. Retighten the bolts.

Now for the fence and miter gauge

Now that the slot is parallel to the blade, set the fence parallel to the slot. I use the right-hand slot to set the fence parallel. Lock the fence down so it is flush to the right side of the right-hand slot at the front of the saw. Then check to see that the fence is flush to the slot at the back end, too. Use your fingers and verify with a straightedge. If both front and back are flush, the fence and slot are parallel and you're good to go. If not, you'll need to adjust the fence. A particular concern is if the fence toes in toward the blade at the back end. This is dangerous because a fence that approaches the blade as it runs front to back puts you at risk of violent kickback. Adjust your fence per the manufacturer's directions and check again.

ADJUST THE GAUGE FOR SQUARE CROSSCUTS

Square the miter gauge. No light should appear between the ruler's edge and the miter gauge's bar while the head of the square is tight to the fence. If it does, loosen the handle and fine-tune the setting.

Test cut confirms your setting. Crosscut a piece of wood with two flat, parallel faces and one jointed edge. With the jointed reference edge against the miter gauge, run the wood through the saw and check the cut with a reliable square.

LEVEL THE TOP FOR
BURN-FREE BEVELS

With the tabletop, blade, and fence parallel, you can true the miter gauge to make 90° cuts. Use your square to verify that the gauge's rod and fence are square.

Dial in the top

Your saw is now set up for clean rips and crosscuts. Sometimes, though, things run awry with beveled cuts, so the last step in the tune-up is to verify that the saw's top doesn't slope up or down from front to back. You won't notice if the table is sloped during 90° cuts, but when the blade is angled, a table that's askew can cause burn marks, poor cuts, and kickback.

Lock down the fence and angle the blade to 45°. You'll need the fence to be exactly parallel to the blade for this procedure. Place a dial indicator against the fence and its plunger against the blade. Zero it out. Pull the plunger away and release it to the same spot to make sure it has been set correctly.

Shim the Top to Align the Blade for Bevels

Even if the blade is parallel with the slots, you may still get burning when cutting bevels. The solution is to tilt the blade and then measure for parallel. If it's off, shim the table at the low end to bring it in line.

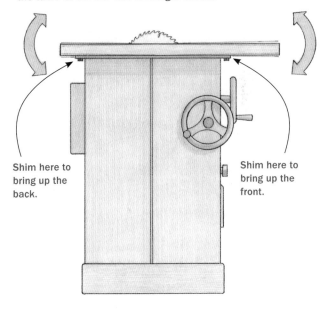

Shim here to bring up the back.

Shim here to bring up the front.

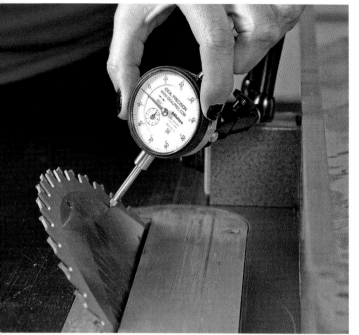

Measure at the front and back. Move a dial indicator along the fence from the front to the back of the blade, rotating the blade so the plunger reads off the same part. If the needle ascends, the tabletop is sloping down toward the back. If the needle descends, the table is rising. The difference should be less than 0.005 in.

Move the indicator along the fence from front to back, rotating the blade so the plunger reads off the same part of the blade. If the needle moves more than 0.005 in., it needs to be addressed. If the needle moves clockwise, shim the back of the tabletop; if it moves counterclockwise, shim the front.

I use thin brass stock from MSC Industrial Supply. The shims go between the tabletop and cabinet. Notch the shims and place them around the bolts to avoid stressing the cast iron, which is very brittle. Use the dial indicator to check your results and reshim as necessary.

These steps may seem finicky, but they're time well spent. After all, once your tablesaw is tuned correctly, you can turn up the volume on your projects to 11.

Shim with brass to align the top. To adjust the top, place one or more notched brass shims around the bolts that secure the tabletop to the base. Remember to retighten the bolts afterward.

Tablesaw Blades for Joinery

BOB VAN DYKE

DADO

BOX-JOINT

FLAT-TOP RIP

DOVETAIL

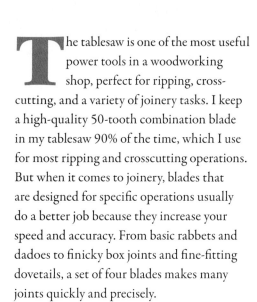

The tablesaw is one of the most useful power tools in a woodworking shop, perfect for ripping, crosscutting, and a variety of joinery tasks. I keep a high-quality 50-tooth combination blade in my tablesaw 90% of the time, which I use for most ripping and crosscutting operations. But when it comes to joinery, blades that are designed for specific operations usually do a better job because they increase your speed and accuracy. From basic rabbets and dadoes to finicky box joints and fine-fitting dovetails, a set of four blades makes many joints quickly and precisely.

The dedicated joinery blades I use most frequently are an 8-in. stacked dado set, a box-joint set, a specially ground flat-top rip blade, and a blade specially ground to cut dovetails. By the way, always invest in high-quality blades; I find they far outperform most cheap blades.

Here I'll show you how to take advantage of these specialty blades to increase the speed and precision of your machine-cut furniture joints.

The secret to perfect splines. The spline jig (left) rides on the tablesaw fence and holds a mitered case or frame. Used in conjunction with the flat-top rip blade, it allows splines to fit all the way into the slots (above) without any gaps.

Dovetail Blade

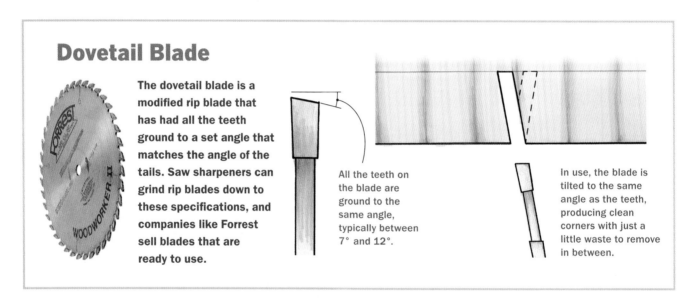

The dovetail blade is a modified rip blade that has had all the teeth ground to a set angle that matches the angle of the tails. Saw sharpeners can grind rip blades down to these specifications, and companies like Forrest sell blades that are ready to use.

All the teeth on the blade are ground to the same angle, typically between 7° and 12°.

In use, the blade is tilted to the same angle as the teeth, producing clean corners with just a little waste to remove in between.

Dovetail blade

A dovetail blade makes cutting dovetails on the tablesaw almost a no-brainer. Almost any blade can be reground by a good saw sharpening service so that all the teeth are at a consistent angle, usually 7° to 12°. The tails are cut on the tablesaw with the blade tilted to match the slope of the dovetail and angled teeth. The pins are cut by hand. Because you are just cutting to a line, you can use any spacing, including asymmetrical. While you can use any blade to cut dovetails, this specially ground blade gives better results because the angled blade cuts right up to the baseline and leaves a flat, clean surface all the way into the corner with little to no cleanup required.

Angle the blade. Because the dovetail blade's teeth are ground to match the angle of the tails (Van Dyke prefers 10°), tilting the blade to that angle results in a flat cut at the base of the tail.

One side first. A jig with an oversize fence holds the piece upright. With the tails laid out, make all the cuts on one side of the tails. For the end, make passes to remove the waste.

To use it, I set the angle of the blade to 10° and raise the blade until it just touches the baseline. If I have set the blade correctly, the top of each cut is smooth and exactly parallel to the baseline and there's very little paring to do. The real advantage of this system, aside from speed, is that each of the tails will come out dead straight and exactly square to the face of the board, which is critical before you can transfer the tails to the pin board.

Flip and finish. Flip the piece edge for edge and make the cuts for the other side of the tails. All that's left after this is to chop out the small amount of waste and cut the pins to match.

Shopmade Tablesaw Inserts

BOB VAN DYKE

The throat-plate insert that comes with most tablesaws can give you headaches. The main problem is that the wide opening doesn't back up the fibers in the wood being cut, which leads to excessive tearout as the blade exits the wood. That big gap also allows small offcuts to fall into the opening and get jammed. And when ripping, thin strips of wood can jam in the gap and kick back very easily. The same can happen with a thin offcut.

The answer to these problems is simple: Use a zero-clearance insert, in which the opening is custom-sized to the blade, eliminating gaps. As a result, wood fibers don't tear out and there is no space to trap offcuts.

While you can buy insert blanks, they can cost a lot. A better option is to make your own. It's cheaper, and you can make one for every blade you might use (standard and thin-kerf, dadoes) and for every common angle (90°, 45°, etc.). The method I'll show you is fast and so easy that you might as well make a dozen blanks to cover every situation. The increased safety and precision will be well worth the short amount of time spent.

Use the stock insert as a template

For the insert material, I use plywood that is a little thinner than the actual depth of the opening, typically ½ in. thick. I prefer Baltic-birch plywood because it's more stable, stronger, and holds the threads I tap into the inserts very well. Make sure the plywood is flat. The first insert I make is always a master blank that all subsequent inserts will be taken from.

To make the master blank, use the stock insert that came with your saw as the template. Using the tablesaw or bandsaw, cut

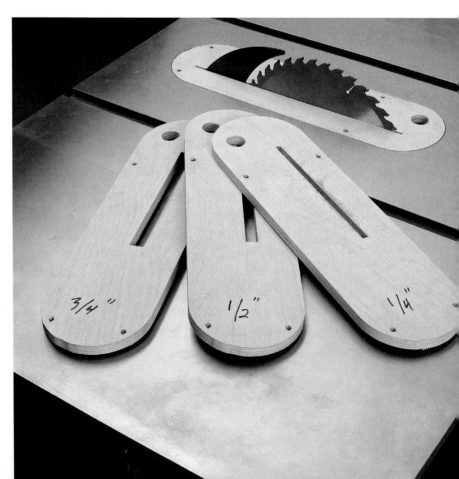

Rough out the insert blank. Use the plate that came with the saw to transfer the outline to the plywood.

a plywood blank about ¼ in. bigger than the insert. Take the leveling screws out of the insert, and trace its profile onto the blank. Transfer the leveling screw hole locations to the blank at the same time. Use a bandsaw to rough out the shape.

Screw the stock insert to the blank using the holes that the leveling screws were in. Use the router table and a flush-trimming

TIP With Van Dyke's method, you can easily make a bunch of inserts at once, enough to cover your standard blade, any common angled cuts, and for the dado sizes you use the most.

Use the original as a routing template. After roughing out the master blank, screw the original insert to the blank. Then use a flush-trimming bit at the router table to get a perfect replica (above left). A wood filler strip in the open end of the insert prevents the bit from catching. Once the master is done, screw it onto another blank to make more insert blanks (left).

bit to rout the blank flush to the insert. The stock insert has a cutout to accommodate the splitter or riving knife. Because the flush-trimming bit could jam in that cutout and kick back, I fill in the opening with a piece of pine and temporarily tape it in place.

After routing, take apart the two pieces and drill a ¾-in. finger hole into the master blank. It should fit easily into your saw's throat opening. Repeat this process using the master blank in place of the stock insert to make as many insert blanks as you need.

Level the insert flush with the table

The new insert must be flush with the top of the tablesaw. In most cases, the ½-in. plywood will be just below the top and will need to be raised flush. For that job, I use ¼-20 Allen leveling screws. I drill and tap through-holes for those screws so that I can adjust the height quickly while the insert is in place.

Knowing where to drill is easy. Just use the holes you drilled to attach the stock insert

Level from above. Predrill the adjustment holes in the insert and then use a tap to make the ¼-20 threads in the plywood.

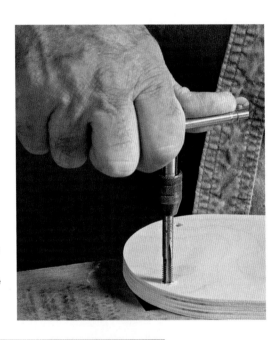

Get the inserts flush with the table. Using a straight rule and Allen key, bring the plate up until it's flush against the ruler and doesn't rock on the adjusters.

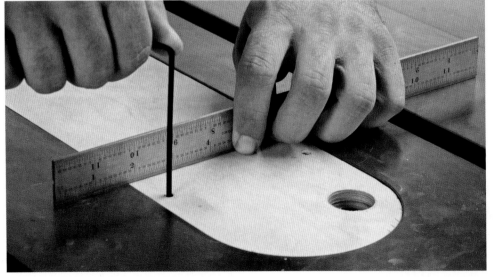

to the plywood blank. Set up a ³⁄₁₆-in. bit in the drill press and drill through-holes in those spots. Tap them using a standard ¼-20 machinist's tap. You may be surprised that you can thread Baltic-birch plywood, but it works great. Thread a ¼-20 by ³⁄₈-in.-long Allen-head set screw into each hole. Remove the blade, install the new insert, and level it.

Cut the zero-clearance slot

When the insert is level, it's time to cut the blade slot. Do this by raising the spinning blade through the insert. Because a 10-in. blade doesn't fit under the insert, I use a single 8-in. dado blade first to create a clearance groove to get the slot started, then change to the 10-in. blade to finish.

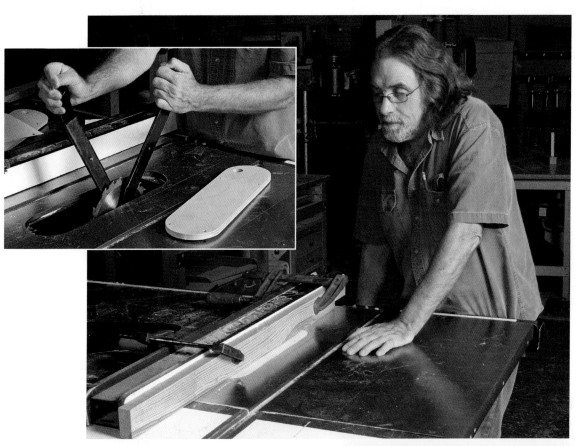

Make way with a dado blade. A standard 10-in. blade won't let the insert sit flat, so use a single blade from an 8-in. dado set (inset above left) to make a clearance slot for a standard 10-in. blade. Clamp a strip of scrapwood to the fence and position it right over the blade (above). The dado-blade kerf should go a little more than halfway through the insert (right).

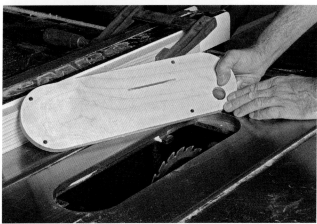

Finishing cut. With the 10-in. blade installed and the scrap block clamped over the blade, raise the blade to its full height to create a perfect zero-clearance slot.

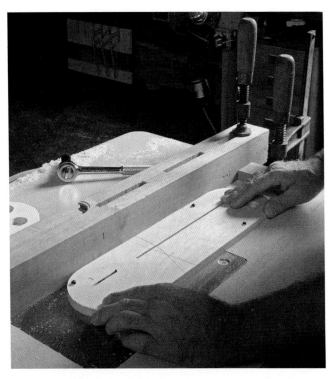

Make room for the riving knife. With a fence and a ⅛-in. spiral bit, extend the kerf from the blade toward the back of the insert to allow for the use of a riving knife or splitter. Use the blade kerf to set up the fence and use a stop block to safely start the plunge cut.

Firmly clamp a piece of scrapwood to the fence and then position the fence so that the scrap is directly over where the blade will come through. This holds the insert down as you raise the blade to full height. It also backs up the cut and minimizes tearout.

Cut the slot for the riving knife or splitter.

For the standard blade insert, you'll need to cut a slot to receive the splitter or riving knife. After marking where it starts and stops, I cut this slot with a ⅛-in. spiral router bit using a router table with a stop attached to the fence.

TIP If your saw doesn't have a splitter or riving knife, you can add a shopmade splitter by routing out behind the blade and gluing in a piece on ⅛-in. plywood. Van Dyke installs an oversize splitter so that when the blade is raised, it will cut the splitter to perfectly match the blade.

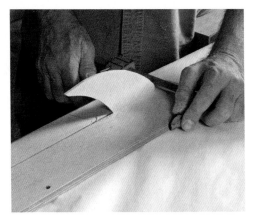

Saws that require special inserts

Some saws use a thin insert. For these, make the standard ½-in.-thick insert in the same way as discussed on p. 27, including drilling the holes for the Allen screws. When you put the insert in place, it will project above the saw table. Measure the amount of projection, add ¹⁄₁₆ in. to that measurement, and then use a router table to cut a rabbet to that depth along the bottom edge of the insert. A ¾-in. rabbet is usually sufficient to clear the adjustment tabs on most saws. The leveling screws will let you raise the insert flush with the saw table.

SawStop brand saws also require a bit more work to be done to the basic insert to clear the arbor washer, a part of the cast-iron trunnion, and the dust-collection shroud. I mapped out the required cuts and holes so you don't have to (drawing, below).

Try making inserts for your saw. Not only will you get cleaner, safer cuts, but you can also see exactly where the blade is cutting— that slot in the insert tells you everything.

Inserts for SawStop Saws

The insert for the SawStop is no different than for any other saw, except for a few clearance cutouts on the underside that allow the blade to raise up fully (top photo, below). Use a Forstner bit or router bit to waste away the wood that is in the way. The drawing below serves as a map. To prevent the insert from tipping, install a short round-head screw in the bottom at the front (bottom photo, below). It bears against a cast-iron ledge and when properly adjusted prevents downward deflection.

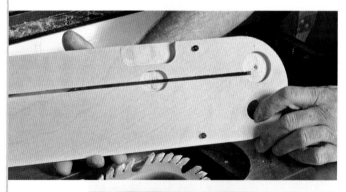

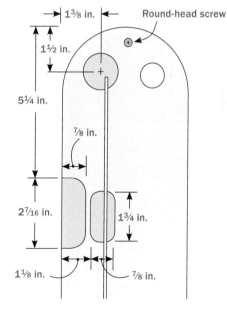

Recesses are ¼ in. deep.

Essential Bandsaw Blades

ROLAND JOHNSON

Bandsaws are the most versatile power tool in many woodworking shops. They can rip, resaw, cut circles and curves, and even crosscut without the risk of dangerous kickback. The key to getting the best results is picking the right blade for each job.

The choices can be confusing. You must understand how the blade width, the number of teeth per inch (tpi), and the tooth geometry all affect the cut you are trying to make. On top of that, you have to consider the wood's thickness. To help you make the right choices, I've come up with a basic set of blades that can perform all of the typical furniture-shop cutting chores. Turns out, three blades are all you really need.

Basic Blade Anatomy

Once you understand how the anatomy of a bandsaw blade affects the work, choosing the correct one for a specific task is easy. Consider the size of the blade and the number and size of the teeth.

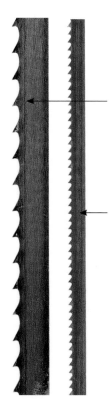

WIDE VS. NARROW

The width of the blade plays a strong role in its performance.

A wide blade won't deflect during heavy cuts, making it ideal for thick rips and resawing, but it can only navigate shallow curves.

A narrow blade can handle those tighter curves without binding, but it will tend to wander on large, gentle-radius curves and circles. It also doesn't have the strength to cut thick material without deflecting or binding.

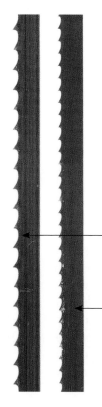

COARSE VS. FINE

The number of teeth per inch (often called the pitch) affects the speed and smoothness of the cut. The basic rule is three teeth in the wood at all times, which prevents the blade from cutting too aggressively for the wood's thickness.

A coarse-pitch blade has fewer teeth, but they're large and cut extremely fast.

A fine-pitch blade has more teeth. Their small size makes for cleaner cuts, but they tend to clog with pitch in thick material.

Tooth Geometry

The shape of a bandsaw blade's teeth is the most critical factor in how it will cut. Understanding these different shapes and when each is most effective will give you better performance from your saw and extend the blade life.

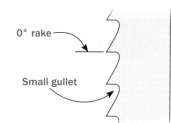

0° rake

Small gullet

REGULAR TOOTH
A regular-tooth blade has evenly spaced teeth with a 0° rake angle. This tooth shape provides clean cuts, but the small gullets clog quickly when moving a lot of dust, so they are not really suited for heavy ripping or resawing.

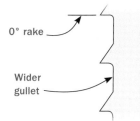

0° rake

Wider gullet

SKIP TOOTH
A skip-tooth blade has a 0° rake angle, like a regular-tooth blade, but every other tooth is essentially skipped. The bigger gullets help clear away dust more effectively.

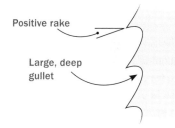

Positive rake

Large, deep gullet

HOOK TOOTH
A hook-tooth blade has a positive rake angle and very large gullets. The teeth cut aggressively and the large gullets evacuate material quickly and effectively. The downside is that the cut surface is rough.

3 Blades Do It All

While the number of combinations possible with different tooth pitch, tooth profile, and blade size is endless, a set of three blades gives you enough versatility and performance to get any job done well. A ⅜-in.-wide, 6-tpi hook-tooth blade, a ¼-in., 10-tpi regular-tooth blade, and a ½-in., 3-tpi hook-tooth blade are all you need in the shop.

ONE FOR GENERAL PURPOSE

ONE FOR CURVES AND THIN STOCK

ONE FOR HEAVY RIPPING AND RESAWING

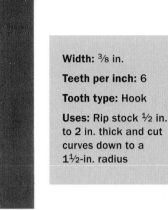

Width: ⅜ in.

Teeth per inch: 6

Tooth type: Hook

Uses: Rip stock ½ in. to 2 in. thick and cut curves down to a 1½-in. radius

1 The all-around blade

While there isn't a single bandsaw blade that does it all, having one that's well suited for a variety of tasks will not only make your day-to-day tasks easier but also will speed up your work. If any blade could be considered all-purpose, a ⅜-in., 6-tpi, hook-tooth, high-carbon-steel blade would be it. This blade has enough width to handle most ripcuts in material up to 2 in. thick without deflecting, but is narrow enough to cut shallow curves. It's also good for quick crosscuts. Following the rule of three teeth in the wood at all times, the 6-tpi blade is best suited for material ½ in. or thicker.

Everyday ripping. The ⅜-in.-wide blade can rip stock from ½ in. to 2 in. thick, depending on the species of the wood.

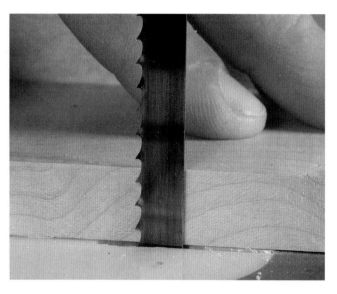

The rule of three. With the 6-tpi all-purpose blade, ½ in. is the thinnest stock you should cut.

Handles curves and straight cuts. The moderate-width blade can work its way around 1½-in. radius curves (above), while still tracking straight lines well (right).

Width: ¼ in.

Teeth per inch: 10

Tooth type: Regular

Uses: Rip stock ¼ in.
to ⅝ in. thick and
cut curves down to a
⅝-in. radius

2 Blade for thin stock and tight curves

While the all-purpose blade is great to keep in the saw for general use, it's too wide to cut truly tight curves and too coarse, or aggressive, for thin stock. My go-to blade for these jobs is a ¼-in., 10-tpi regular-tooth blade.

With this blade, tight curves as small as ⅝-in. radius are a piece of cake. And the fine teeth provide a clean cut, especially in thinner material—you'll be able to cut ¼-in.-thick stock without it splintering or tearing out. Sawing curves, especially circles, is more about crosscutting than ripping, which results in fine, short-grained sawdust. Despite the small size of the gullets, they adequately clear that dust.

Ripping thin. The narrow cross-section of this blade and the regular tooth profile make it ideal for ripping thin stock and leaving a clean cut in its wake.

Thin, but not too thin. In keeping with the "three-in-the-cut" rule, ¼-in. stock is the thinnest you'll want to go for best results.

Match the Blade to the Curve

A ⅜-in.-wide blade can tackle most curves, but a ¼-in.-wide blade can go tighter still.

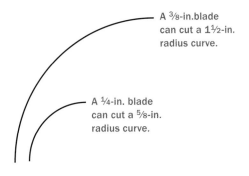

A ⅜-in.blade
can cut a 1½-in.
radius curve.

A ¼-in. blade
can cut a ⅝-in.
radius curve.

Take the curve. This blade's narrow cross-section allows it to take turns as tight as a ⅝-in. radius cleanly and without shuddering.

Width: ½ in. to ⅝ in.

Teeth per inch: 3 to 4

Tooth type: Hook

Uses: Rip stock at least 1 in. thick and resaw up to 6 in. (½-in. blade)

Resaw up to 12 in. (⅝-in. dedicated resaw blade)

3 Blade for thick stock and resawing

Another task at which bandsaws excel is resawing and ripping thick stock. The thin blade has a smaller kerf than a tablesaw and there's no danger of kickback. Ripping wood creates lots of stringy sawdust that easily packs the small gullets of an all-purpose blade, robbing the saw of power and keeping the teeth from easily cutting into fresh wood. The best choice for ripping is a ½-in., 3-tpi hook-tooth blade. The aggressive teeth and big gullets of this blade cut fast and evacuate a lot of dust quickly. Because of the low teeth per inch, 1-in. stock is the thinnest stock you should cut with this blade. For heavy cuts, a blade must have sufficient beam strength to resist deflection when force is applied to its cutting edge. The ½-in.-wide blade works well for cutting stock from 1 in. to 6 in. thick (or wide for resawing).

Handling a heavy cut. This blade's big gullets and coarse teeth mean that ripping thick stock is fast and easy.

Three's plenty. This blade is best used with stock 1 in. and thicker, to keep three teeth in the cut and get the best performance from the blade.

For those who do a lot of resawing of stock or veneers, a dedicated resaw blade can be a great addition to this set. A ⅝-in., 3- to 4-tpi variable-pitch blade is perfect for clean, accurate cuts in thick or wide material (up to 12 in.). A variable-pitch blade's fluctuating tpi count helps eliminate the vibration that is often produced when working with thick stock.

For blade material, I prefer high-carbon-steel blades for ripping domestic wood, bi-metal for abrasive wood, and carbide for really nasty stuff like jatoba. For resawing, I prefer a true carbide-tipped blade like the Laguna Resaw King. If that's out of your price range, the carbide-impregnated SuperCut Wood Saver Plus is also a great option.

Ready to resaw. In addition to the fast-working teeth, the ½-in.-wide blade is strong enough to handle most resaw jobs without deflecting, such as resawing a board for drawer fronts.

Master big resaws. If you do a lot of resawing, a carbide-impregnated or carbide-tipped blade can provide superior longevity and a better-quality cut in extra-thick stock.

Make Your Blades Last

You'll get poor results with a blade that's dirty or dull. When the gullets get lined with pitch, the blade has an increasingly hard time evacuating dust. As a result, you need to use excessive force when feeding the wood, causing the blade to wander or the thrust bearings to lose their setting.

I scrub dirty blades with a brass brush (left; make sure to turn the wheel counter clockwise by hand as you clean), and I also thoroughly clean roughsawn boards before cutting them (below). A dull blade will also cause problems. If you need to push harder to make cuts, if the blade starts to drift consistently in one direction or wander, or if you notice increased burning or smoking, your blade is dull.

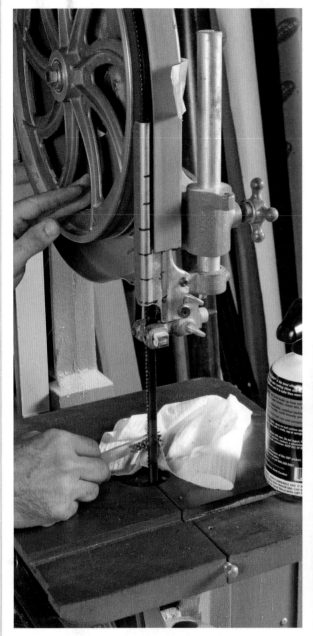

Drill Presses

WILLIAM PECK

While a benchtop drill press will be adequate for the majority of holes you drill, there will be times you'll want the power and capacity of a full-size machine. On average, floor-mounted drill presses offer more power, larger tables, and more swing (the distance between the post and the chuck). Most importantly, many of today's machines have 4-in.-plus of quill travel (the distance they can plunge a drill bit), which not only makes deeper holes possible but also means you won't have to adjust the table height as often—still an awkward process on any drill press. Finally, a floor-mounted drill press might actually save space in your shop, by sitting in a corner vs. taking up valuable countertop space.

Drill presses haven't evolved far from their machine-shop roots, so I focused on models with two woodworker-friendly features: quill travel of at least 4 in. and a table that tilts 45° in both directions. That narrowed an enormous field to nine machines from six manufacturers. (JET, Powermatic, and Shop Fox had machines that fit our criteria, but they declined to participate.) Chucks ranged from ⅝ in. to ¾ in., all plenty big for woodworking bits. All came prewired for 120 volts.

Narrowing the Field

Most drill presses are designed for machinists, so we insisted on these two woodworker-friendly features.

Extra quill travel. We looked for at least 4 in. of travel, for mortising this big trestle foot, for example.

Table tilt. Machines with at least 45° of table tilt allow angled holes like those in this Windsor chair seat.

Clean, consistent holes of any size

The main reasons I choose a drill press over a handheld drill are power and precision, so I looked at those attributes first. To test power, I used a 2-in.-dia. high-speed steel (HSS) Forstner bit to drill through 2 in. of hard maple. I used Lee Valley and Veritas bits for all the tests, as they have done very well in *Fine Woodworking*'s past tool tests.

I ran the bit as close to the recommended 400 rpm as each model allowed, and I drilled with a very heavy hand. I wasn't able to stall any of the motors, but I was able to make the belts slip on a couple—the Porter-Cable and the General International 75-700—even after pulling the belts extra tight. That meant

I couldn't push this big bit quite as hard on these machines. However, that would only be a problem if you were drilling scores of big holes a day. All of the machines produced very clean holes, by the way.

To test runout and accuracy, I tightened ¼-in.-dia. and ½-in.-dia. drill rod (precisely ground lengths of drill steel) in the chuck, placed a dial indicator against the rod, and turned the chuck slowly by hand, letting go before taking each reading. In case the chuck's grip was inconsistent, I remounted the rods several times and repeated the test, averaging the results. Runout ranged between 0.001 in. and 0.005 in. We rated anything under 0.003 in. as "good" or better.

To see how this slow-moving test would be reflected in actual performance, I drilled ¼-in.-dia. and ½-in.-dia. holes in soft pine, plunging the bits slowly to allow for any runout to affect the hole diameter. I then removed the drill bit from the chuck and inserted the shank end into the hole, looking for looseness. All of the machines did much better on this real-world test. The ¼-in. shank fit snugly in all of its holes, while the ½-in. holes had only minor looseness—around 0.001 in. for all machines except the Porter-Cable, where I found an extra 0.001 in. of wiggle, which is still very acceptable. And all produced clean results, even at the rim of the hole.

I combined the dial-indicator test and the drilling test into one runout rating, shown in the chart on pp. 46–47.

Two Stand-Out Machines

Delta
18-900L

Porter-Cable
PCB660DP

A Delta bonus. The Delta is the only machine with a usable table insert. It is leveled via set screws, and you can screw into it from below to hold it down.

DELTA 18-900L

The Delta 18-900L was a no-brainer for the Best Overall award. It has the most quill travel, a big table that tilts in both directions, the fastest and easiest speed changes, a quick-adjust depth stop and quill lock, an effective head-mounted laser pointer, and plenty of power and accuracy.

PORTER-CABLE PCB660DP

At one-third the price of the Delta, the Porter-Cable PCB660DP is the most affordable machine in the test and an easy pick for Best Value. It offers a quick-adjust depth stop and quill lock, a good laser pointer, and easy speed changes. The table is small, with a rim that is ¼ in. below the center section (making it hard to clamp at the edges), so you will definitely want to add an auxiliary table. But at $320, this machine is a steal.

One table stood out

The variously sized cast-iron tables were not a concern, as most people will place some sort of plywood or MDF auxiliary table on top of theirs to prevent tearout on the bottom of holes. All of the tables have mounting slots for this purpose.

However, with its large overall size, flat edges for clamping, and unique table insert, the Delta's table works fine on its own. The replaceable insert sits on set screws, which not only keep it level but also allow dust to get onto the ledge below without lifting the insert.

Timed test for power. Peck drilled through 2 in. of maple with a 2-in.-dia. Forstner bit. All the machines handled this tough test well, but elapsed time varied.

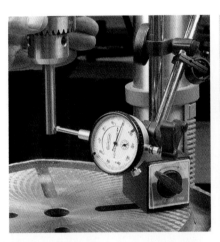

Measured and real world. To test drilling accuracy, Peck used a drill rod and a dial indicator (right), turning the chuck by hand. Then he drilled a series of holes and inserted the drill shank (far right) to check for oversize ones.

Front-to-back squareness. With a piece of flat MDF on the table to even out inconsistencies, Peck placed a square against the drill rod. A few tables had a bit of sag, but the one from Central Machinery (shown) had a lot.

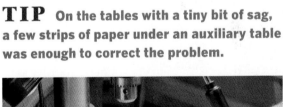

TIP On the tables with a tiny bit of sag, a few strips of paper under an auxiliary table was enough to correct the problem.

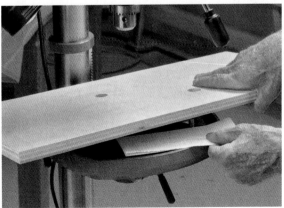

Speed changes separate the pack

While smallish bits can all be run at a similar speed, anywhere between 1,000 and 2,000 rpm, bits bigger than ½ in. dia. should be run in the 500 to 1,000 rpm range, and some very large Forstner bits and wing-cutters should be run even more slowly. So you will be changing speeds pretty often.

The time needed to make speed changes varied considerably among machines. In theory, the two variable-speed units would shine here, but the General International 75-700 still requires a belt change to get from a lower speed range to an upper one, and that belt change is tedious, thanks to set screws that require an Allen wrench and a long motor-cover screw that must be completely unthreaded

The other eight machines require a belt change for each speed setting, but on most, this took only a minute or less.

Other points to consider

To drill to a specific depth, or just to avoid drilling into the cast-iron table, you'll need to set the depth stop. Eight of these units uses a rod with an adjustable stop to limit depth. The adjustable stop is a nut that you spin by hand, but on three models—the Delta, the Porter-Cable, and the Rikon—the nut has a quick-release button that lets you make big adjustments rapidly.

The Central Machinery has the ring near the crank handle that adjusts depth. This also works well.

While laser pointers are not necessary, I preferred those on the Delta and Porter-Cable machines, which are wired to the machine and mounted on the head. The others are battery-operated and mounted on the post, so if the head of the machine shifts you'll have to re-align the lasers.

Variable speed is fastest, but . . . On the General International 75-700 variable-speed machine, speed changes happen in seconds. But they still require a belt change between a high and low range.

Best of the belts. With a quick-release tension roller, the Delta's belts were the fastest to change by far.

Quick-adjust depth stop. The Porter-Cable, Delta, and Rikon machines have a quick-release button on their depth stops as shown here. Others make you spin a nut (or a dial) for big adjustments.

Spindle lock. Most machines have a way to lock the quill at various heights, which is a must when using a sanding drum. The Delta and Porter-Cable do it with another quick-release button, which is handy.

Delta table tilt is unique. It is the only machine that allows front-to-back table adjustment as well as the usual side-to-side, making compound angles possible as well as correcting table squareness.

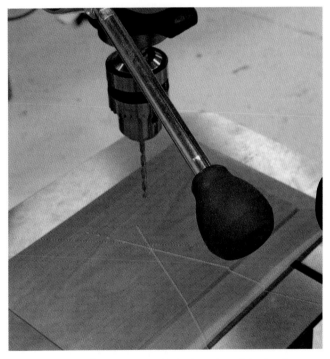

Lasers are not always an asset. Peck preferred the head-mounted lasers that are hard-wired into the machines, like those on the Delta and Porter-Cable (shown). These are less likely to shift out of alignment than column-mounted models.

Central Machinery 39955

Delta 18-900L — BEST OVERALL AUTHOR'S CHOICE

General International 75-260 M1

General International 75-500

General International 75-700 M1 VS

MODEL	PRICE/ WARRANTY*	MOTOR	SPEEDS/RANGE	SWING	QUILL STROKE	TABLE SQUARENESS (FRONT TO REAR)
Central Machinery 39955	$560/ 90 days	1½ hp	12/ 180–3,865 rpm	20 in.	4¾ in.	Fair
BEST OVERALL AUTHOR'S CHOICE Delta 18-900L	$1,030/ 5 years	¾ hp	16/ 170–3,000 rpm	18 in.	6 in.	Adjustable
General International 75-260 M1	$760/ Lifetime	1 hp	12/ 255–2,750 rpm	17 in.	6 in.	Excellent
General International 75-500	$1,200/ Lifetime	1 hp	12/ 120–2,270 rpm	17 in.	4½ in.	Excellent
General International 75-700 M1 VS	$2,100/ Lifetime	1 hp	VS/280–1,140 and 800–3,200 rpm	22 in.	5⅞ in.	Excellent
Grizzly G7947	$575/ 1 year	1 hp	12/ 210–3,300 rpm	17 in.	4¾ in.	Very good
Grizzly G7948	$695/ 1 year	1½ hp	12/ 210–3,300 rpm	20 in.	4¾ in.	Excellent
BEST VALUE AUTHOR'S CHOICE Porter-Cable PCB660DP	$320/ 3 years	¾ hp	12/ 300–3,100 rpm	15 in.	4 in.	Very good
Rikon 30-240	$1,050/ 5 years	1 hp	12/ 180–3,865 rpm	20 in.	4¾ in.	Excellent

* Check with manufacturers for limitations.

Grizzly
G7947

Grizzly
G7948

AUTHOR'S
BEST VALUE
CHOICE

Porter-Cable
PCB660DP

Rikon
30-240

RUNOUT	AVERAGE SPEED CHANGE	POWER TEST**	QUILL LOCK	WORK LIGHT	COMMENTS
Good	1 min.	10 sec.	Yes	Poor	Weak work light, too much table sag front to back.
Excellent	30 sec.	11.5 sec.	Yes	Good	Best table, easiest belt changes, quick-release depth stop, only machine with front-to-back table adjustment.
Good	2 min. 50 sec.	11 sec.	No	None	Good accuracy but tedious process for changing speeds.
Good	2 min.	11 sec.	No	Very good	Good accuracy, very good work light, useful low-end speed, but difficult belt changes.
Good	Variable, 2 min. range change	12 sec.	No	None	Accurate, but two variable-speed ranges require troublesome belt change.
Fair	1 min. 5 sec.	8 sec.	No	Very good	Tied for most power, very good work light.
Very good	1 min. 10 sec.	8 sec.	No	Very good	Tied for most power, very good work light.
Good	53 sec.	19 sec.	Yes	Very good	Good accuracy, great conveniences, low price.
Very good	1 min.	13 sec.	Yes	Very good	Very accurate, with quick-adjust depth stop and very good work light.

** Average time needed to drill 2-in.-dia. hole through 2 in. of hard maple.

What Drill Bits Do You Really Need?

ROLAND JOHNSON

No matter what kind of woodworking you are doing, eventually you'll have to drill a hole in something. Tasks can range from drilling pilot and clearance holes for screws to mortising for chair legs. There are a few basic requirements for drilling accurate, concentric holes: The bit must create a clean entry, run concentrically so that it produces an accurate bore, and have appropriate cutters and geometry for the material being cut. Finally, it should clear away waste during the cut.

There are many types of drill bits out there, and it can be tough to make the right choices, especially if you're just starting out as a woodworker. But don't worry. I've been woodworking for decades, and I've drilled holes in all sorts of materials and in every situation imaginable. So here I'll give you some time-tested guidance on which bits you need and why. Before I get to the recommendations, though, here's some money-saving advice.

I purchase bits in sets because it's a good value. Buying a single bit gets expensive, especially if shipping costs are involved, and invariably the one bit you don't have will be the one you urgently need in the middle of

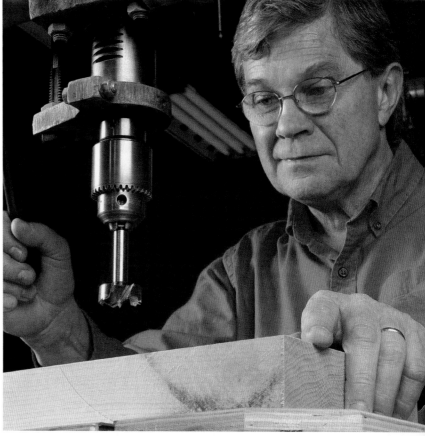

a project when time is of the essence. Yes, I have bits that have never been captured by a drill chuck and may never be, but having full sets of bits in my shop, ready for use, gives me peace of mind. Another big advantage to buying sets is that most come with a case that will keep your bits organized and protected. By the way, all of the drill-bit sets I'll talk about here are readily available at most woodworking-supply stores.

Brad-point bits

Brad-point bits look like slightly modified twist bits. The bit has spurs machined on the tips of the flutes (some designs simply have the tips sharpened at an angle, resulting in a point at the outside edge) and a centering spur that is slightly longer. The spurs cleanly shear the fibers and the helical flutes efficiently transport waste from the bore. Brad-point bits create clean bores both on entry and during the cut.

Brad-point bits have a downside. They aren't very good at drilling end grain cleanly. They will cut most angled holes cleanly and efficiently, but if the angle is too shallow (5° to 10° off center), you won't get good results.

Clean and easy. Brad-point bits make a very clean entry, leave clean hole walls, and don't wander at the start or during a cut. They are perfect for shelf-pin holes that will be visible and must be precise.

Superior chip ejection. Ideal for peg holes, the brad-point bit removes chips as you go. Use a tape flag stop (left) when you don't need to be ultraprecise. But use a wooden stop (above) when you need to prevent the bit from breaking through the other side.

Twist bits

A jack of all bits, the common twist bit does a good job at cutting a variety of materials—wood, plastics, and sheet goods. However, these bits excel at drilling shallow, small-diameter holes in wood (for hinges and hardware) and for drilling clean holes in end grain.

There are limitations, too. First, unless you're cutting into end grain, these bits leave some tearout. Twist bits also can meander at the start of the cut if there isn't a starter hole or center point for the bit to register in. Plus, they're not great at evacuating chips because of their rather small flutes, and they tend to scorch the wood, on occasion creating enough heat to damage the bit. That means they're not great for deep holes—use brad points for those. Twist bits also are not good for cutting flat-bottomed holes or drilling at angles over 45°.

TWIST BITS

13-piece set, 1/16 in. to 1/4 in.

Twist bits are superb for use in all hardwoods and metals, except hardened steel. High-speed steel (HSS) bits are the best general-purpose bits.

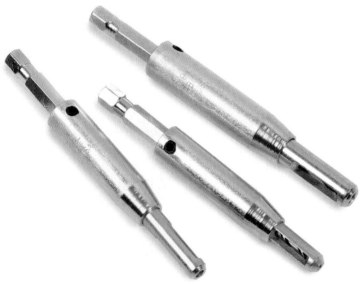

VIX BITS

3-piece set for screw sizes 5 through 10

Twist bits with a spring-loaded sleeve are used for drilling centered holes for hardware.

COUNTERBORES

5-piece set for screw sizes 5 through 10

These three-in-one bits drill clearance holes, pilot holes, and counterbores all at once for installing flat-head screws.

Follow the leader. Because of its web, or V-angle point of the bit, a twist bit is the bit of choice for drilling multiple steps because it follows the center of a predrilled hole or the centerpoint a Forstner bit leaves.

Center perfect. A Vix bit has a spring-loaded sleeve that surrounds a twist bit. The beveled end of the sleeve automatically aligns the bit to the center of the mounting hole in the hardware.

Another variation on the twist bit. The counterbore bit is an all-in-one bit for screws. Combined with a countersink and depth stop, the tapered twist bit does an exemplary job of drilling holes that allow the screw head to be flush with the surrounding wood.

Forstner bits

The ideal wood-cutting bits, Forstner-style bits circumscribe the rim with a slicing cutter and follow the scribe with low-angle shearing wings that leave a flat, clean bottom and a smooth wall. They can be used effectively for overlapping holes and can produce clean, accurate angled holes even when the bit enters the board at a steep angle.

A drawback with Forstner-style bits is the lack of chip extraction in deep bores. As the bore deepens, the chips tend to clog around the bit shank. If the bit isn't retracted from the bore at regular intervals, the detritus packs tight, sealing the bit in the bore.

Toothed Forstner-style bits are excellent for boring large holes. Sawteeth cut into the rim do an effective job of shearing the end grain, and gullets between the teeth help control the debris. Toothed bits cut much faster than a continuous-rim Forstner but don't leave as crisp a shoulder.

FORSTNERS

7-bit HSS Forstner set (¼ in., ⅜ in., ½ in., ⅝ in., ¾ in., ⅞ in., 1 in.)

When buying a set, stick with smooth-sided bits.

Big holes are no problem. Forstner bits make a clean entry and don't wander during the cut, so wider holes are easy. Make sure to back the bit out of the hole frequently to clear the waste, or the bit will jam in the hole and burn the wood.

Steep angle overachiever. Forstner bits excel at cutting severe angles accurately and cleanly. Just be sure you give the workpiece solid support.

Partial holes are easy. MDF scrap offers additional protection against tearout and helps register the bit.

Benchtop Planers

KELLY J. DUNTON

I've had a benchtop planer in my shop for many years and it's starting to show its age. So when the editors at *Fine Woodworking* asked me to test the current crop of benchtop planers, I saw it as an opportunity to do some comparison shopping. These models handle stock 12½ in. to 13 in. wide (plenty for most furniture making) and 5 in. to 6 in. thick, so you can square up blanks for even the beefiest parts. The planers also run on a 120-volt circuit, so they can be used in any home shop.

There are a lot of benchtop planers on the market, but we limited our selection to the 10 models that have what we consider to be essential features: dust collection and indexed knives. Planers without a dust port will create a huge mess and flood the air with dust. Indexed knives have pins that guarantee that all of the knives project the same amount and are parallel to the planer's bed. This feature takes the hassle out of knife changes, greatly speeding up the switch from old to new knives.

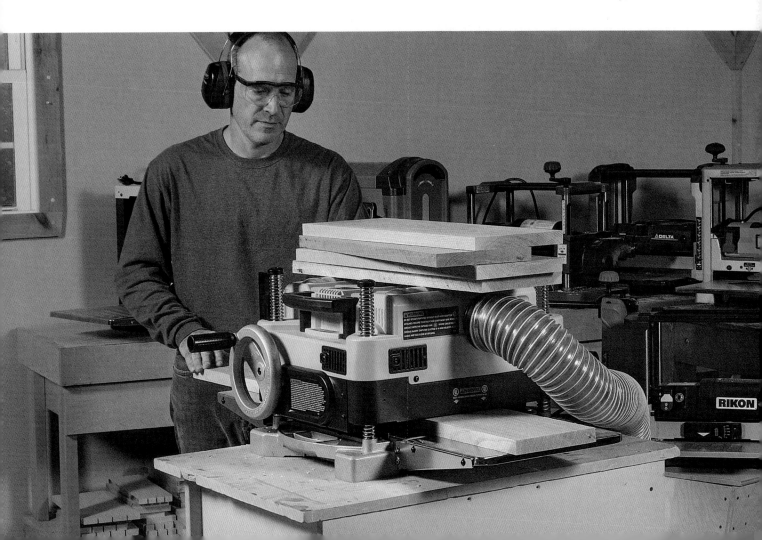

The curly maple challenge. All of the planers we tested handled white oak and white pine without trouble, but only the two DeWalt machines and the Ridgid planer produced usable finished surfaces on curly maple.

To test the planers, I looked at what matters most to woodworkers. I ran a wide board through each one to determine if it planed the surface parallel to the one that ran on the bed. I measured for snipe, a planer's tendency to cut a bit deeper at the leading and trailing ends of board than in the middle. I also evaluated the quality of the surface each machine produced.

My tests showed that all of the machines were suitable for woodworking, but the machines with three knives produced the best surfaces. Also, the two machines with segmented cutterheads performed about as well as those with two knives. I think this is because the cutters entered the wood straight on, just like straight knives. All the machines are loud. You'll need hearing protection when using any of them.

Parallelism and snipe. A planer's job is to make two faces parallel to one another, and any machine that leaves surfaces more than 0.01 in. out of parallel is going to give you headaches. As for snipe on the ends, more than 0.01 in. is too much.

Make it fast. Changing knives should be easy so that you can quickly get back to work. DeWalt embedded magnets into the handle of its wrench, making it a snap to lift old knives and put new ones in place.

However, the planers were not all equal, and three were better machines than the rest. The DeWalt 735X clearly was the Best Overall. With a three-knife cutterhead and two planing speeds, it produced nearly glass-smooth surfaces, even on curly maple. It left very little snipe and had outstanding dust collection, and the knives were dead-on parallel to the bed. Two other machines did very well, the DeWalt 734 and the Ridgid R4331. Both have three-knife cutterheads and produced very good surfaces, but with some tearout on figured woods. The Ridgid costs $30 less than the DeWalt 734, so it's my pick for Best Value.

Give it a twist. The insert cutters on the General International and Rikon segmented cutterheads can be turned to a fresh edge without completely removing the screw that holds them in place.

Convenience is king. A depth-of-cut adjustment wheel on the side is easy to reach. Three of the machines have side-mounted wheels, but this convenience doesn't trump surface quality.

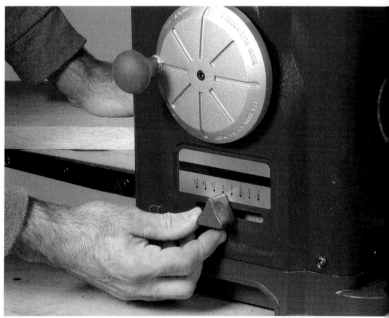

Depth stops simplify repeat milling. Stops for common thicknesses make it a snap to mill parts to the same thickness, a handy feature when you need to remake a part. All the stops tested were accurate.

DeWalt 735X

The DeWalt 735X produced two faces perfectly parallel to one another, with surfaces far superior to what the other machines produced, thanks to its two feed speeds. At high speed, the planer works fast and leaves a smooth surface. But the slower, finish speed produces an almost glass-smooth surface. Knife changes are easy, with spacious access to the cutterhead from the top and a gib screw wrench that doubles as a magnetic lift to remove the knives. The 735X also has great dust collection, thanks to an internal blower that helps evacuate chips. The port has a 2½-in.-dia. opening but has a built-in adapter for 4-in.-dia. hoses. My only complaint is the location of the dust port: It's on the outfeed side of the machine and exits straight back. If you don't pull the hose to the side, it interferes with material as it leaves the machine. The top is large and flat, so it's a great place to set material in between passes through the machine.

Price: $649
Warranty: 3 years
Knives: 3
Size: 13 in.
Depth stops: 6
Snipe: 0.003 in.
Out of parallel: 0.000 in.

Dust collection: Excellent
Noise level: 102 db.
Surface quality
  White pine: Excellent
  White oak: Excellent
  Curly maple: Very good

Ridgid R4331

Priced nearly $300 less than the DeWalt 735X, the Ridgid R4331 is an excellent value. Its three-knife cutterhead left wonderfully clean surfaces on plainsawn white oak and white pine. It did not perform nearly as well on curly maple as the 735X, but it created less tearout than all but one of the other machines (the DeWalt 734 was its equal). Knife changes were quick and easy with the provided T-handle wrench. Dust collection was good, assisted by an internal fan. The 2½-in.-dia. port on the outfeed side of the machine is directed to the side, so the hose is out of the way. The planer's top is flat and provides a good surface for holding stock between passes.

Price: $369
Warranty: 3 years
Knives: 3
Size: 13 in.
Depth stops: 8
Snipe: 0.003 in.
Out of parallel: 0.005 in.

Dust collection: Good
Noise level: 100 db.
Surface quality
  White pine: Excellent
  White oak: Excellent
  Curly maple: Good

Triton TPT125

Accessing the knives on the Triton for changes was not difficult, but getting the knives out was tricky, because no magnetized handles were provided to lift the knives off the cutterhead. There is a 2½-in.-dia. dust port, and chip collection was good when hooked up to a shop vacuum. The housing has an open top and just one return roller on top, making it impossible to stack boards there in between passes through the machine. Also, there is no gauge that indicates how much material you are removing in a pass, making it one of four planers that don't offer this feature.

Price: $426
Warranty: 1 year
Knives: 2
Size: 12½ in.
Depth stops: None
Snipe: 0.101 in.
Out of parallel: 0.01 in.

Dust collection: Good
Noise level: 102 db.
Surface quality
  White pine: Good
  White oak: Good
  Curly maple: Poor

Delta 22-555

Knife changes on this planer were easy enough, except that you need an Allen wrench to open the dust cover and gain access to the knives, and it's not the same size as the wrench used to loosen the screws that secure the knives. The 2½-in.-dia. dust port can be reversed for use on either side of the machine. Two material rollers on top of the machine aid with transferring stock from the outfeed side back to the infeed side. Finally, there is no gauge that indicates how much material you're about to remove, a convenience that three other planers also lack.

Price: $339
Warranty: 5 years
Knives: 2
Size: 13 in.
Depth stops: None
Snipe: 0.006 in.
Out of parallel: 0.008 in.

Dust collection: Good
Noise level: 98 db.
Surface quality
  White pine: Good
  White oak: Good
  Curly maple: Poor

Dewalt 734

One of only two machines with a cutterhead perfectly parallel to its beds, the DeWalt 734 is a very good planer. Knife changes overall were straightforward, but access is difficult because you must remove a Phillips-head screw from under the dust shroud— not an easy task. The dust port on the back of the machine has a 2½-in.-dia. opening but can be hooked up to a 4-in.-dia. hose. Connected to a dust collector, it did an excellent job gathering chips. And because the port exits to the left of the machine, the hose is never in the way of exiting boards. The top of the machine is flat, making it a good place to stack boards between passes.

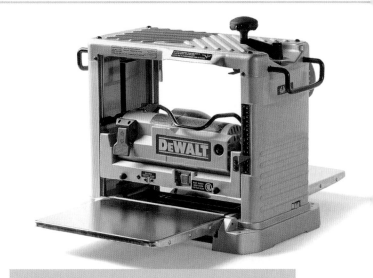

Price: $399
Warranty: 3 years
Knives: 3
Size: 12½ in.
Depth stops: 4
Snipe: 0.002 in.
Out of parallel: 0.000 in.

Dust collection: Excellent
Noise level: 102 db.
Surface quality
  White pine: Excellent
  White oak: Excellent
  Curly maple: Good

General Intl. 30-060HC

The General International is one of two planers in the test with a segmented cutterhead (the Rikon 25-130H is the other). The 26 cutters, arranged in six rows, enter the wood straight on. Each cutter has two cutting edges and can be rotated to get a fresh edge. However, rotating and changing out the cutters is a bit tricky because there is no cutterhead lock, so it tends to move as you loosen and tighten the screw for a cutter. A dust chute on the outfeed side of the machine has both a 2½-in.- and 4-in.-dia. port, one exiting to each side. The top of the machine is large and flat, a great place to rest boards between passes.

Price: $700
Warranty: 3 years
Cutters: 26
Size: 13 in.
Depth stops: 8
Snipe: 0.002
Out of parallel: 0.008 in.

Dust collection: Good
Noise level: 101 db.
Surface quality
  White pine: Good
  White oak: Good
  Curly maple: Poor

Grizzly G0790

Knife changes on the Grizzly planer were tricky, because access was tight, the screws were small, and the Allen wrench provided was hard to use. The machine has a single dust port that's not a standard size, and I needed tape to connect a hose to it. Two rollers on the top of the machine make returning material to the infeed side easy, and they're stable enough that you can stack boards on them, too. The Grizzly is one of four planers that do not have a gauge indicating how much material is about to be removed on the next pass through the machine.

Price: $285
Warranty: 1 year
Knives: 2
Size: 12½ in.
Depth stops: None
Snipe: 0.004 in.
Out of parallel: 0.013 in.

Dust collection: Fair
Noise level: 99 db.
Surface quality
  White pine: Good
  White oak: Good
  Curly maple: Poor

Makita 2012NB

Of the planers with two-knife cutterheads, the Makita produced the best surface quality. The knives are very narrow and a bit tricky to change, but Makita provides two magnets for lifting them off the cutterhead, and these make it easier. The machine's dust port is an odd size, with an outside diameter of approximately 2⅞ in. I used an adapter to connect it to a 4-in.-dia. hose, but dust collection was only fair. Finally, a full revolution of the height-adjustment wheel moves the cutterhead ³⁄₃₂ in. The other machines move ¹⁄₁₆ in. with a complete revolution of the handle, a dimension that's much easier to work with because the most common thicknesses for furniture are in multiples of ¹⁄₁₆ in.

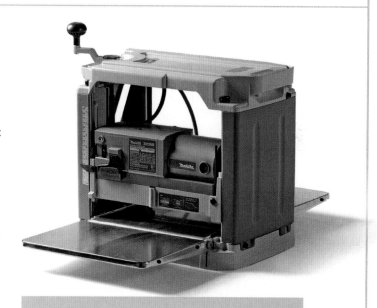

Price: $546
Warranty: 1 year
Knives: 2
Size: 12 in.
Depth stops: One, but it's adjustable
Snipe: 0.003 in.

Out of parallel: 0.002 in.
Dust collection: Fair
Noise level: 98 db.
Surface quality
  White pine: Very good
  White oak: Very good
  Curly maple: Fair

Rikon 25-130H

The Rikon 25-130H, like the General International 30-060HC, has a segmented cutterhead with 26 cutters arranged in six straight rows that enter the wood straight on. Rotating and changing the cutters was easier on the Rikon than on the General International, because it has an automatic cutterhead lock. There is a flat top that is a good staging area for boards between runs through the machine. There are two dust ports on the back of the machine (2½ in. and 4 in. dia.), with one exiting on either side of the planer. Dust collection was good with the planer connected to a 4-in.-dia. hose and dust collector.

Price: $650
Warranty: 5 years
Cutters: 26
Size: 13 in.
Depth stops: 8
Snipe: 0.003 in.
Out of parallel: 0.001 in.

Dust collection: Good
Noise level: 99 db.
Surface quality
   White pine: Good
   White oak: Good
   Curly maple: Poor

Craftsman 21758

The knives on this planer were easy to access, and springs underneath the gib lift it up so that you can remove the knife without removing the screws. The 2½-in.-dia. dust port can be oriented to exit on either side of the machine. This planer's cutterhead was significantly out of parallel and the snipe was bad. The top of the machine has a single stock roller, so you can't rest boards there between passes. Because of a little tab molded into the cutterhead's housing, you cannot take off more than 1⁄64 in. with a single pass unless your stock is narrow enough to pass through on either side of the tab. The Craftsman also is one of four planers without a gauge that indicates how much material is about to be removed.

Note: At the time of publication, this product had been discontinued.

Price: $303
Warranty: 1 year
Knives: 2
Size: 12½ in.
Depth stops: None
Snipe: 0.012 in.
Out of parallel: 0.019 in.

Dust collection: Good
Noise level: 96 db.
Surface quality
   White pine: Good
   White oak: Good
   Curly maple: Poor

Track Saws

MARK EDMUNDSON

Clamps optional. The tracks for these saws have a nonslip grip, so you should be able to place them on your mark and simply make the cut. But for added security, all the saws offer clamps as an option. The clamps slide into a groove on the bottom of the track to lock it down.

I was one of the first people to review the Festool 55 track saw when it came on the market, and I went around for several years afterward telling all my woodworking friends to buy the tool. The magic of the track saw is in the track, which has a nonslip surface underneath and a zero-clearance strip along the edge. In seconds, you can line up that edge with your layout marks, drop the saw onto the track, and make a perfect cut, right on the line. Add the ability to plunge in and out of a cut and you have a truly unique tool, unmatched at a number of tricky tasks that range far beyond its original mission: cutting up sheets of plywood for cabinet work.

Since my first review, other manufacturers followed Festool into the market, and *Fine Woodworking* thought it was high time for a lowdown on the whole lot. We reached out to all of the manufacturers and netted seven saws for our test. Shop Fox and Scheppach declined to participate.

Saw and track combinations vary a bit, so in each case we ordered the saw with a track at least 48 in. long, because a track saw should be able to crosscut a sheet of plywood. And for some insurance on critical cuts, we also ordered the accessory clamps that lock the track to the workpiece.

What I tested and why

To evaluate the power and quality of cut, I used the saws to cut through a wide variety

Break down sheet goods. If you work with sheet goods, you'll appreciate the track saw's ability to come to the work. Instead of wrestling a plywood sheet onto a tablesaw, you can slide it onto sawhorses and cut without breaking your back or damaging the sheet. The saw also tilts for easy bevel cuts.

Put a straight edge on lumber. You can cut at any angle, so you can put a straight edge on crooked boards or align an edge with the grain.

Trim doors and drawer fronts. You can even use the saw to fit a door or a panel into an opening.

of thick hardwoods—ripping 8/4 maple and oak and 4/4 alder and crosscutting a 1½-in.-thick maple butcher block. I also took a skim cut on the edge of the butcher block to check for blade deflection, and I cut a variety of veneered sheet goods. All of the saws produce clean edges under their zero-clearance strips, and the best deliver a clean edge on the outboard side of the kerf, too. I also noted the smoothness of the plunge action and how comfortable the handle was.

Some of the saws set the depth in metric units and others in imperial, but I didn't find the measurement units to be a big issue. However, I do like the fact that some saws factor the track height into the depth measurement.

I find track saws to be very useful when cutting bevels. To test their accuracy, I used the saws to cut two long 45° bevels in plywood to see if the joint would close with no gaps. In the process, I evaluated the bevel gauge for accuracy and readability. Some of the saws have a catch that prevents the saw from tipping off the track when bevel cutting, a handy feature.

Dust collection is tricky on track saws, where the hose tends to catch on things as the saw moves. That's why some of the saws have dust ports that can be positioned at a certain angle and will stay there, keeping the hose away from the track and the edge of the material. All of the ports fit the smaller-size vacuum hoses.

Festool TS 75 EQ
$780 with 75-in. track, plus $80 for two track clamps

BEST OVERALL AUTHOR'S CHOICE

Festool TS 75 EQ

The Festool TS 75 EQ was the powerhouse of the lot, blowing right through the thickest, toughest materials, and with an unmatched 3-in. depth of cut. There was no blade deflection, cuts were very smooth, and the track side of the blade kerf was super-clean. Bevel cuts were very clean and accurate, but it can't bevel below 0° and there is no stop at 45°—minor inconveniences. The trigger is easy to engage, and the plunge action is the easiest of any saw in the test. The depth-setting adjustment is also the easiest to use, but you have to factor in the track height. The dust collection is efficient. The track did not slide and is long enough to crosscut a sheet of plywood (longer tracks are available, too). The strips on the edge of the track are translucent so that you can keep better track of your pencil line. The Festool clamps are the best, and they fit everything except the DeWalt and Mafell tracks.

Power. To compare the saws' power, Edmundson made ripcuts on 2-in.-thick oak and hard maple, timing each cut. The Festool 75 powered through without slowing.

Some of the saws have a riving knife behind the blade and others don't. I didn't find those to be a factor on track-guided cuts, but they are helpful if you use the saw without the track, like a normal circular saw, to crosscut a big piece of rough lumber, for example. However, these saws are awkward to use without the track. You have to push forward while also pushing down.

All of the tracks I tested are capable of reaching across a full sheet of plywood, but some extra length is convenient, because you don't have to be so precise when positioning the track and you have room to plunge the saw fully before pushing it forward to cut.

Conclusions

I have two picks for Best Overall: the Mafell and the Festool 75. For value shoppers, I recommend the Makita. It might take a little fussing with the settings to get it to cut perfectly, but once you do, it offers clean cuts, good power, and easy adjustments.

Mafell MT55CC
$870, plus $154 for 63-in. track
and $62 for two track clamps

BEST OVERALL AUTHOR'S CHOICE

Mafell MT55CC

The Mafell is compact and powerful, with a motor that was by far the quietest and smoothest. The surprising power might have something to do with its blade, which is the narrowest in the group (but did not deflect in the skim test). The quality of the cuts was also excellent in all materials. Accuracy was just as good, with the 45° bevel joint closing up nicely. And the track is a standout, too, tied for stability with the Festool tracks. We went with the 63-in. model, as the next size down is under 4 ft. long. The track stayed put during the slip test. The depth setting is one of the easiest to change, and, like the Triton, the scale factors in the track height. There are accurate bevel stops for both 0° and 45°, and the saw can also tilt past those settings. The dust collection was the most efficient of any saw in the test.

Track length. Edmundson opted for the 63-in.-long track on the Mafell, which lets you plunge the saw fully, with the saw fully engaged in the track, before entering the cut on a full sheet of plywood.

BEST VALUE AUTHOR'S CHOICE

Makita SP6000J1

The Makita is not as polished as the Festool or Mafell tools, but it is comfortable to use and performed very well. Power was very good, slowing only in the 8/4 hardwoods. After some adjustment to make the blade parallel to the baseplate, it delivered clean cuts in all materials. Like the Triton, the Makita has a tab on the base that keeps it from tipping off the track when tilted for bevel cuts, and the saw can tilt past 0° and 45°. The bevel scale is not accurate, but if you make some test cuts, you can set the positive stops at 0° and 45° accurately, which is mostly what matters. The plunge action was smooth with a comfortable handle angle. Dust collection was good, and the track did not slide under pressure.

Makita SP6000J1
$410 with 55-in. track, plus $40
for two track clamps

Bevel cutting. Track saws do a great job cutting long bevels if you keep them steady. The Makita (shown) and the Triton have a little clip on the base that keeps the saw from tipping off the track.

DeWalt DWS520SK

The DeWalt had no problem in ¾-in.-thick stock but really bogged down in 8/4 oak. It left a smooth cut and a clean edge under the track, the blade showed no deflection, and the measurements are in inches. However, unlocking the trigger to plunge the saw is an awkward experience, and the depth setting is a bit cumbersome to adjust and doesn't factor in the track thickness. The dust port was difficult to pivot but it did a good job at collecting dust. The 55-in. track is longer than most of the others and is the only one to allow cutting on both sides. The track slid under pressure, but the DeWalt clamps work well and will fit all of the tracks except the Mafell.

DeWalt DWS520SK
$475 with 59-in. track, plus $32 for two track clamps

Festool TS 55 REQ

The Festool TS 55 REQ has less power than some of the other saws, but the trigger is easy to engage, and the plunge action is the easiest of any saw in the test. The depth-setting adjustment is also the simplest and easiest to use, but you have to factor in the track height. The saw has positive bevel stops at 0° and 45° and allows for -1° and +45° settings. There was no blade deflection, and cuts were very clean, even when beveling. Dust collection is very efficient. The Festool clamps are the best, and they fit everything except the DeWalt and Mafell tracks.

Festool TS 55 REQ
$660, plus $130 for 55-in. track and $80 for two track clamps

Grizzly T25552

The Grizzly's plunge action was much too stiff, and the angle of the handle and locations of the trigger and lock made the saw difficult to use. The blade deflected when taking a skim cut, and the saw rocks on the track a little bit, causing inconsistencies in the bevel cuts. The track slips easily and the dust collection is not very effective. On the positive side, the depth setting is straightforward and uses standard measurements, and the bevel gauge is easy to read.

Grizzly T25552
Master Pack $260, includes 55-in. track and two track clamps

Triton TTS1400

The Triton's cuts were not as smooth as those made by the top-performing saws. The plunge action was stiff, and there was some blade deflection when making skim cuts. The depth setting uses an inconvenient twist knob, and there are no positive stops on the bevel adjustment. The dust collection was not very effective, and the track moved. On the plus side, the track clamps worked well, and the saw features a tab that keeps it from tipping when making bevel cuts. Also, the depth gauge reads in inches and factors in the track thickness.

Triton TTS1400
$315, plus $85 for 59-in. track and $50 for two track clamps

Add Bushings to Your Router Kit

JEFF MILLER

Routers are among the most versatile tools in the shop once you learn to control them, and one of the most versatile ways to gain this control is with guide bushings. These surround a router bit and provide a bearing surface that works with all kinds of shopmade templates and commercial jigs, making it easy to cut mortises, tenons, pockets for inlay, dovetails, dadoes, and sliding dovetails. More complex templates can include multiple joints, so you can rout all of the mortises in a chair or bed leg at one time.

The bushing itself is a metal tube attached to a plate. The predominant style of bushing is the one originated

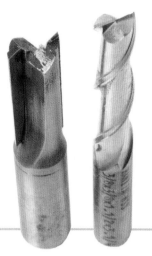

Two Options for Straight Bits

Normal straight bits (right) are less expensive and work fine for most tasks, but I prefer spiral bits (far right). They cut more cleanly, draw chips out of deep mortises, and have bottom cutters that extend to the center point, so they can plunge more easily.

by Porter-Cable, which can be used in a number of different brands of router. A few companies have base designs that require their own bushings. Some routers allow for adjusting the guide bushings to be sure they are perfectly concentric to the router bits. Mine don't, so I make sure to keep the orientation of the router consistent as I work.

The key to working with guide bushings is understanding the offset between the bushing and the bit. A straight router bit must be smaller than the inside of the bushing. Calculating the difference between the out-side diameters of the bit and the bushing and then dividing that number in half gives you the offset. For example, with a ½-in. bushing and a ⅜-in. bit, the offset is 1⁄16 in. Pay attention, though, because in many cases, you need to subtract this offset from both sides of a cut.

The art of template-making

There are many kinds of templates and many good ways to make them, depending on your tools, the materials you have lying around, and the task at hand.

Most bushings need a trim. For the bushing to work with thin templates, you should saw off some of the excess length. Leave ¼ in. to ⅜ in. to engage the template.

Attachment varies by router. The most common style is the Porter-Cable, which is held in the base of the router or an adapter by a threaded ring (left). Bosch's bushings are even easier to use, dropping into a spring-loaded holder (right).

Easy-to-Make Template

Mortising is one of the best tasks for bushing-guided routing, and there are many ways to make a template. This one is built around the bushing from individual pieces of solid wood, leaving a perfect pocket in the middle to guide the bushing.

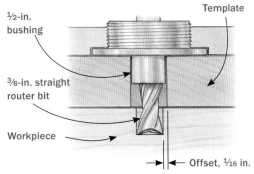

½-in. bushing

Template

⅜-in. straight router bit

Workpiece

Offset, ¹⁄₁₆ in.

FACTOR IN THE OFFSET
The bushing diameter is larger than the bit, so the cut will be offset from the edge of the jig. The difference in diameters divided in half is the offset.

Cut the center strip into three sections to create an opening for the bushing. Plane the middle section a bit thinner than the ends.

The position of the fence will determine the location of the mortise. Be sure to factor in the offset when attaching the fence.

Rip a board into three strips. The width of the center strip should match the diameter of the guide bushing.

I'll cover two of my favorite methods here. The first method is building up the template from separate pieces of solid wood, glued together and guided by the bushing size. I also sometimes cut slots in plywood or MDF. Because MDF is softer, you may want to toughen up the reference edges by painting them with thin cyanoacrylate glue.

The first step in designing your template is to calculate the offset. Then you'll want to determine the overall size of the template. It needs to be large enough to fully support the router base. Figure in a little extra width and/or length so that you can clamp the template to the workpiece without interfering with the router.

Build the base. Rip a strip from the center of a flat board, chop that strip into shorter pieces, and reassemble the parts to leave a pocket in the middle. The goal is a slot that fits the bushing perfectly, so clamp the parts together to check (top). Use a spacer when gluing up the base to be sure the pocket is the right length, but don't glue it in (above).

Add the fence. Make the fence wide enough to extend from the edge of the template to the edge of the workpiece (don't forget the offset). Clamp it in place, feeling with your fingers to keep the outside edges flush (left). Then flip it over and drive screws (right).

Mortising is job one

Mortising with a guide bushing is almost foolproof. It's useful if you need to cut mortises in the same location on various workpieces, and it is an excellent option for parts that are oddly shaped, such as chair components. Mortising is also a good way to learn the basics of bushing-guided routing.

I'll start with the mortises in a table leg. In this case, I'll build the template from separate solid-wood pieces to show how easy that is. Let's use a ⅜-in. straight bit with a ½-in. bushing, a typical combination for mortising, yielding a ⅜-in.-wide mortise at any length you need.

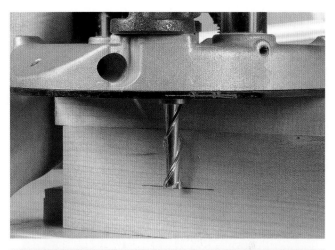

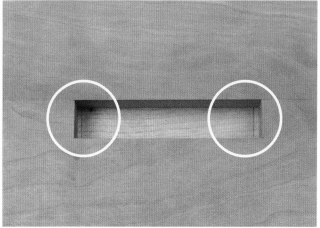

Set up for mortising. Bring the edge of the template to the edge of the workpiece, then extend the bit down to a line that represents the desired mortise depth and lock it there (above right). You only have to mark the ends of the mortise to locate the jig accurately on the workpiece (right).

Mortising tips. Plunge the router ⅛ in. or so between passes. Deeper plunges will cause the bit to wobble slightly and cut an oversize mortise. Also, be sure to keep the router oriented the same way throughout the process. If the bushing is slightly out of line with the bit, the offset will vary when you twist the router, changing the path of the cut.

Keep it clean. Mortises will become packed with chips, so pause occasionally to vacuum or blow them out. For the final pass, vacuum out the last chips, and clean up the mortise, pushing the bushing along each wall in case there is a little slop in the slot.

A template built in pieces. Start by ripping all the pieces from a single flat board. Rip a ½-in. (or slightly wider) strip from the middle, and then plane it to the same size as the bushing. Cut this strip into three pieces, with the center portion ⅛ in. longer than the desired mortise to account for the offsets on either end. Plane this middle piece a little thinner; it will be a spacer strip to control the length of the mortise opening in the jig.

Now glue the two big side pieces to the two outer middle strips. Put the thinner middle strip in place, but don't glue it (you might even wax it a little). When the glue is set, push the spacer strip out of the jig.

Then joint and/or plane the template to make it flat.

Next, attach a fence on the bottom of the template. Account for the bit offset when locating it, and clamp it in place before screwing it down, to keep it from shifting. I don't use glue, so I can relocate the fence as needed for other mortising jobs.

Tips for bushing-guided mortising

Clamp the template in place where needed and set the depth limit on the router. You can do this by measuring or by placing the router on the template so that it hangs over

Jig for Dadoes and Dovetails

This template makes flawless dadoes, sliding dovetails, and combinations of the two. Make it by sawing a partial slot in a piece of plywood and attaching a fence at the open end.

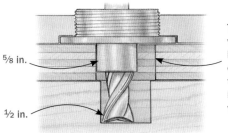

5/8 in.

1/2 in.

The 7/8-in. slot is wider than the bushing in this case, in order to let a 1/2-in. bit cut a 3/4-in.-wide dado.

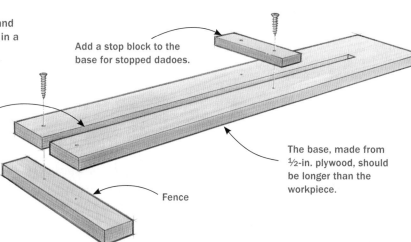

Add a stop block to the base for stopped dadoes.

The base, made from 1/2-in. plywood, should be longer than the workpiece.

Fence

Making the jig. To start, cut the slot and add a fence. Make long cuts (left), turning off the saw at the end of each cut, and then remove the waste with a jigsaw. Clamp the fence square to the slot and screw it in place (above).

Stops are easy to add. For stopped dadoes, screw down a block to stop the router in the right spot.

Rout a stopped dado. Use the notch in the fence to line up the jig with your layout marks (above). Push the router up the left side of the jig and then pull it back along the right side to keep the bushing tight to the walls of the slot on both sides (right). Square the ends of a stopped dado with a chisel.

the edge and allows you to set the depth directly from the workpiece.

Take multiple shallow passes and the work will go quickly.

Unless your mortise is quite shallow, you'll soon find that the bit is trapping wood shavings, limiting the router's movement. Stop to clear away the chips with a shop vacuum or a blast of air as needed.

When you get to the bottom of the mortise, clear the chips one more time and make a last clean pass at full depth, pushing gently against all sides of the template opening. Don't lift the router off the template until you've raised the bit up out of the cut and it has come to a complete stop.

Now you can move the template onto any part of your table leg to make identical mortises wherever you need them.

Dadoes without do-overs

To cut consistent dadoes without worrying about variations in size or any chance of the bit wandering, I use a two-sided fence that captures the bushing on both sides. This leaves the bit nowhere to go but straight. For this type of template, I typically use a single piece of plywood, making long stopped cuts on the tablesaw until I have the exact width I want (the width of the desired dado plus the two offsets). Then I cut out the waste piece with a jigsaw. At the stopped end of the slot, I leave enough plywood to keep the whole template stable. At the open end, I screw on a fence, being careful to keep the fence perfectly square to the slot.

The first time you rout a dado with this jig, the router bit will cut into the fence, and that notch will give you an exact indication of where to align the jig. Just line up the cut in the fence with your layout marks.

Rout a Dovetail Slot

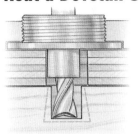

Use a straight bit to remove most of the waste before dovetailing.

Start with a straight bit and follow with a dovetail. Plow out a dado just narrower than the narrow part of the dovetail you'll be cutting (above). Follow with the dovetail bit. It helps to have a second router set up with the dovetail bit, so you don't have to change bits and lose your depth settings for each (right).

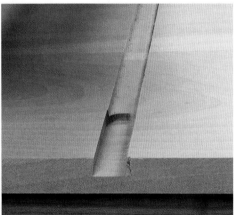

Combining dadoes and dovetails. After plowing the dado, drop in a strip to set the length of the sliding dovetail (left). This handy stop goes in and out easily between dadoing and dovetailing. The jig ensures that the sliding dovetail is perfectly centered on the dado, and accurate in length (above).

You can add stops anywhere along the opening by screwing down blocks to stop the router base.

The dado jig is perfect for sliding dovetails, too, with the same advantages over a single fence. The dovetail bit will cut more easily and accurately if you first plow out most of the waste with a straight bit. Then switch to the dovetail bit and finish up the cut.

Multi-joint template tames complex projects

Once you get the hang of working with guide bushings, you'll be able to work out your own ways to take advantage of the accuracy and control they give.

One of my favorite techniques for complex workpieces is to make a large template with multiple joints included in it. This locks

One Jig to Do it All

You can combine multiple joints into a single template for anything from a chair leg to an entire case piece. The one shown here is for the sides of a small chest of drawers with three drawer dividers and two rails dovetailed into the top edges.

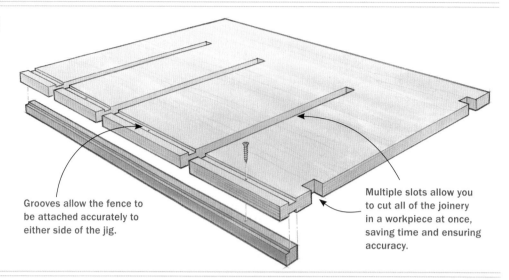

Grooves allow the fence to be attached accurately to either side of the jig.

Multiple slots allow you to cut all of the joinery in a workpiece at once, saving time and ensuring accuracy.

in the joint locations. I use these multi-joint templates for the sides of case pieces (for dadoes, sliding dovetails, and half-blind dovetails) and the back legs of chairs (multiple mortises), among other tasks.

Master the basics of guide bushings, and you'll find many other applications for this indispensable router technique.

Dadoes and dovetails. This jig lets Miller cut a combination of long, shallow dadoes and short dovetail slots in three different spots on a solid-wood case side.

Make it reversible. The fence on this big jig has a shallow tongue that fits into matching grooves on either side, so it can be flipped for two opposite sides of a case.

Dust Collection for the Small Shop

ANATOLE BURKIN

The importance of dust collection cannot be overstressed in woodworking. But honestly, it's tough to get excited about spending money on tools that, well, collect dust. No matter how fancy, these machines just don't have the cachet of sleek hand tools or powerful machines that cut and shape wood.

The good news is that a basic kit of dust-collection products won't cost a fortune. And whether you're doing woodworking in a basement or garage, building projects large or small, the essentials are the same. In my case, I'm remodeling a house—trimwork, cabinets, and built-ins—and working out of a two-car garage. The materials I'm using range from rough lumber to sheet goods.

To make things more difficult, I live in a community with strict homeowners' association rules that prohibit turning a garage into a permanent workshop. So at the end of the day (or a few days running), I need to be able to park the motor vehicles back in the shop . . . er, garage. And to keep from tracking lots of dust into the house, I've gotten into the habit of keeping the garage pretty clean with minimal effort.

Three-Pronged Approach

When it comes to managing dust, treat the various machines and tools in your shop differently based on how much dust they create. For stationary machines like the jointer, planer, tablesaw, and bandsaw, use a dust-collection system. But for smaller, handheld tools like the circular saw or orbital sanders, a shop vacuum will do the trick. Round up whatever's left circulating with an overhead air filter.

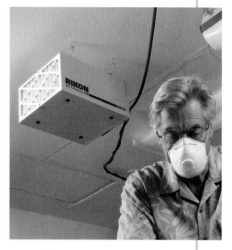

DUST COLLECTORS
The wider diameter hose and large air volume created by a dust collector make it the right choice for big machines that create a lot of large, heavier sawdust particles and chips.

SHOP VACUUMS
The smaller volume of fine dust created by chopsaws, routers, and sanders can be handled by a shop vacuum.

OVERHEAD FILTRATION
A ceiling-mounted air filter can grab the finest particles that end up suspended in the air. A dust mask is a good idea, too.

In the end, no matter what size shop you're in, a three-pronged approach is the best way to attack dust before it settles on you and everything around you. Use a dust collector for bigger, stationary machines, a shop vacuum for handheld tools, and round things out with an overhead air filtration system combined with a dust mask.

Go big for bigger machines
It's tempting to think that a good shop vacuum can solve all dust-collection issues. That might be true when working with only small benchtop tools that don't include a jointer and planer. But if your woodworking

TIP Don't let the bag get too full. Empty the bag before it's completely full (shoot for about a third from the top of the bag) to prevent clogging and to keep the dust from spilling out during the change-out.

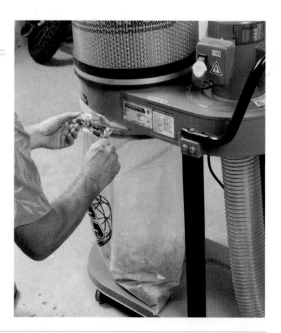

involves milling rough lumber, a jointer and planer (or a combo machine) are absolutely essential, and so is a dust collector. Jointing and planing wood produces large, heavy sawdust particles, and to move them, a fairly large amount of air volume (about 350 cfm) as well as a 4-in.-dia. hose are required. Shop vacuums aren't suitable for a job that big.

A dust collector is also more capable of grabbing sawdust from a tablesaw and bandsaw, again because of the large volume of airflow. That said, I've had pretty good luck using a shop vacuum hooked up to a 14-in. bandsaw and a benchtop tablesaw that has a built-in dust housing under the blade. For larger machines, and especially if you plan to do a lot of resawing or dadoing, the dust collector would do a better job than a shop vacuum, whose hose can sometimes clog when taking big cuts.

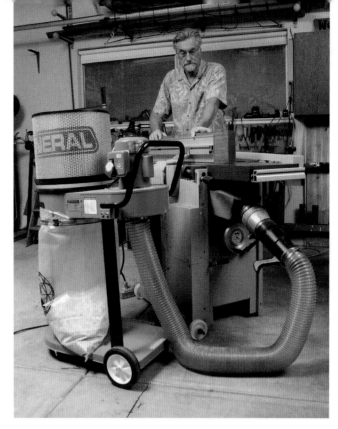

Keep your collector close to the dust. When using a small dust collector, typically a machine with about 1 hp, use a fairly short hose, about 10 ft. long. Too long a run of hose reduces the airflow, and the result is ineffective dust collection as well as possible jams.

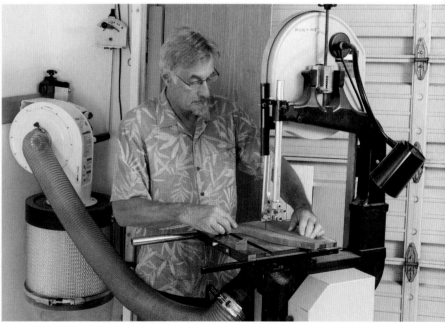

When floor space is tight. Though it can weigh about 65 lb., a wall-mounted dust collector can be moved quickly (it just hangs on a bracket) and stored elsewhere if needed. Get an extra wall bracket or two and move it around the shop where it's needed.

Easy hose attachments. Whether they're spring loaded or the thumbscrew type, toolless clamps and fittings are immediately accessible using only your fingers. The thumbscrew type hold a bit tighter than the spring clamps, but the latter are the fastest to get on and off when switching between tools.

For this chapter, I tried two 1-hp dust collectors that would fit my small space: a mobile tool (General International model No. 10-030CF M1) and a wall-mounted machine (Grizzly Industrial model No. G0785), each with pleated filters. Both were up to the task and handled every situation presented in my shop.

To keep the costs down and get the most cfm at the tool, forget about ductwork and blast gates. Just hook up the dust collector to one machine at a time.

Quick and easy change. Rockler's Dust Right handle and tool ports speed up swapping a 4-in. hose from machine to machine. Once the ports are installed on each machine, the handle slips snugly over the open end, requiring no tools or clamps.

Downsize for smaller power tools

Power sanders create very fine dust and are good candidates for a hookup to a shop vacuum.

Chopsaws, routers, and biscuit joiners also can be handled by a shop vacuum, which can generate close to 100 cfm. Finer and fewer dust particles don't require as much air volume. That said, chopsaws are pretty messy no matter what's hooked up to them because most have not been designed with highly effective dust-capturing capability.

From a workhorse basic to bells and whistles. While a sturdy, no-frills model is great to have, a handy feature on higher-priced vacs is the auto-start function. When a power tool plugged into the vacuum is turned on, the vacuum starts automatically.

Adapt and Connect

Most shop vacuum manufacturers have dedicated adapters that make changing from one tool to another easy. Get a brand that fits your vac.

Narrow hose works better. The 2½-in.-dia. hose that comes with a typical shop vacuum is too large in diameter for easy hookup, plus it is stiff and bulky. Invest in a smaller-diameter hose, which allows for easier hookup and more freedom of movement.

When using hand tools such as chisels and handplanes, the chips and shavings produced are relatively large and won't get airborne. A broom and dust pan can handle the job just fine, although I've become fond of a floor sweeper that attaches to a dust collector. It captures both the large chips and fine sawdust left behind from other tools.

Powered air filters finish the job

In spite of one's best attempts to control the mess, some dust always escapes and the finest particles can end up suspended in the air. For that, I recommend a ceiling-mounted air filter. Now, some experts say that these machines circulate dust particles while they are running, a time during which your lungs may be exposed to more dust (vs. quiet air, when dust tends to settle). So to be really safe, it makes sense to wear a respirator or dust mask when dust is in the air. Or, run the air cleaner during a break when you're not in the shop.

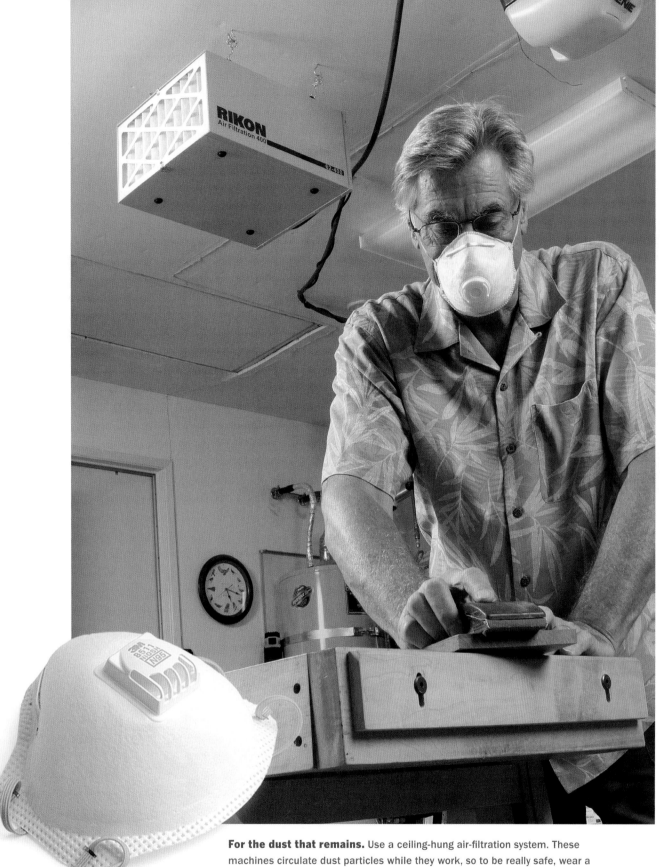

For the dust that remains. Use a ceiling-hung air-filtration system. These machines circulate dust particles while they work, so to be really safe, wear a respirator or dust mask when dust is in the air.

A note about dust collectors and filters

There's a lot to learn about the various types of dust collectors and filters, and for more on the topic, check out "A Revolution in Dust Collection," *Fine Woodworking* #223 (*Tools & Shops* 2012).

But to cut to the chase, here are the key points:

■ For respirators, use one rated for fine particles (N95 rating) as the last stand against sawdust.

■ Use high-efficiency filters on all dust-collection devices (dust collectors and shop vacuums) that capture particles down to 1 micron or less. These small particles can enter deep into the respiratory tract past the body's natural defenses.

■ The cartridge-style filters you see pictured on the single-stage dust collectors in this article are a big improvement over the bags typically supplied with budget dust collectors. Cartridge filters have a large surface area, which allows the machine to breathe better (improving airflow), and include internal flapper arms, which allow the user to brush off dust inside the cartridge, keeping them operating more efficiently.

Basic Dust Collection Kit

1-HP DUST COLLECTOR
$300–$400

14-GAL. SHOP VACUUM
$100

AIR CLEANER
$190

ACCESSORIES
$100

PART TWO

TECHNIQUES

The Physics of Machine Safety

TODD BRADLEE

It was only after many years of working wood—and one big scare—that I began to think seriously about machine safety and developed a real understanding of the forces at work when a spinning blade or bit cuts a piece of wood. In this chapter I'll show you how to compensate for those forces and control the workpiece as

you work at the tablesaw, bandsaw, jointer, drill press, and router table.

My awakening came 17 years into my career. I began working as a carpenter at 18, and I saw some pretty frightening things on job sites. Carpenters seem fond of running blades within an inch or two of their fingers. After 14 years in the building trades, I was burned out but unscathed.

Two-handed tablesaw technique. Your left hand, anchored near the edge of the table, applies downward pressure and keeps the workpiece against the fence. Push the workpiece through the blade with your right hand (left). To keep your right hand well clear of the blade, start using a push stick when your hand reaches the table (above).

Having found inspiration in some custom furniture I had seen, I began to design and build furniture. Three years later, at age 35, my right hand was pulled into a tablesaw blade by a kickback. The blade nicked the tip of one finger, but otherwise I was unhurt. I was very fortunate, but luck doesn't last, so I began to study the machines I used daily. I wanted to understand how they cut, so I could use them more safely.

Tablesaw

The tablesaw presents the most complex challenge to maintaining control. You must keep the workpiece moving forward, flat on the table, and pressed against the fence. Failing to do any one of these three things can result in serious injury. Fortunately, a pair of hands and a push stick are all you need to combat those forces and stay in control. Past the blade, the workpiece engages the splitter, which helps keep the board against the fence.

Tablesaw Cutting Forces

Back side of blade lifts workpiece off table.

Rotation of blade pushes workpiece back.

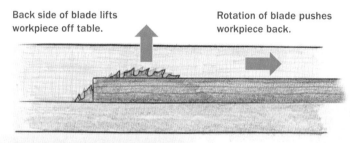

If the feed pressure is not in line with the force exerted by the blade, another force comes into play, causing the workpiece to pivot away from the fence.

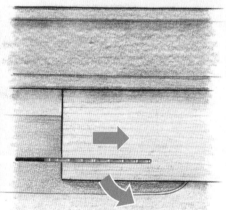

HOW TO CONTROL THEM
Push workpiece into blade.

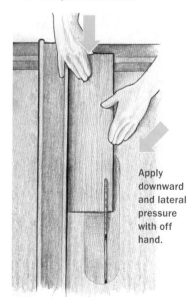

Apply downward and lateral pressure with off hand.

Placed out from the fence, a push stick can keep a workpiece moving forward while holding it down on the table and tight against the rip fence.

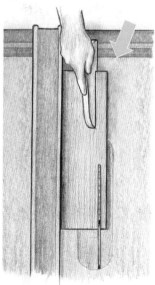

Thin slices. When taking thin slices, beware of a wandering blade. When ripping or resawing, a blade cutting near the surface of a workpiece can quickly veer off course and out of the wood, so use a push stick.

Bandsaw Cutting Tendency

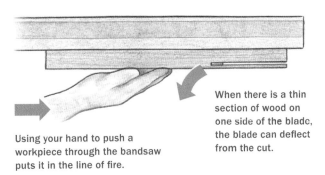

Using your hand to push a workpiece through the bandsaw puts it in the line of fire.

When there is a thin section of wood on one side of the blade, the blade can deflect from the cut.

HOW TO COPE WITH IT

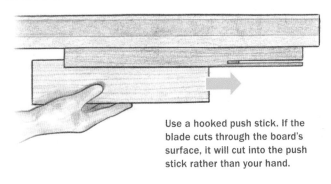

Use a hooked push stick. If the blade cuts through the board's surface, it will cut into the push stick rather than your hand.

Bandsaw

As it cuts, a bandsaw blade exerts downward force that pushes the workpiece onto the table. This is fine as long as the part you are cutting is flat. Things get a bit tricky when the workpiece is curved and only contacts the table at one point. If you keep that point of contact right in front of the blade, you'll be OK. When cutting thin slices from a board, use a push stick to protect your hand in case the blade wanders from the cut and out of the board.

Curved work. For curved work exploit the blade's motion to improve control. The blade forces the workpiece onto the table. Keep the point of contact right in front of the blade, and the downward force will help steady the workpiece.

Bandsaw Cutting Force

Because it cuts on the down stroke, a bandsaw blade pushes the workpiece against the table.

A curved piece above the table at the point of the cut can be violently pushed down.

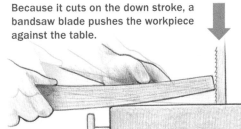

HOW TO CONTROL IT

Keep the workpiece on the table at the point where it's being cut.

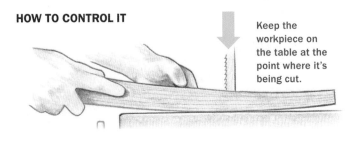

Press down and push. Use your left hand to keep the board flat on the jointer's table while pushing it forward with your right hand.

Jointer Cutting Forces

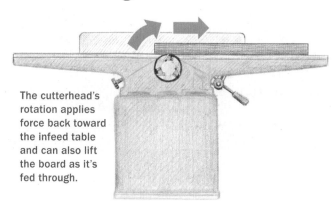

The cutterhead's rotation applies force back toward the infeed table and can also lift the board as it's fed through.

HOW TO CONTROL THEM

Don't push forward with your lead hand. It could come off and into the cutterhead if the board is thrown back by the cutterhead.

Your lead hand should apply downward pressure only.

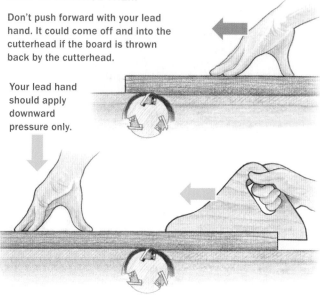

Jointer

As it spins toward the infeed table, a jointer's cutterhead pushes the workpiece back toward you as you feed it across the knives. At the same time, the cutterhead exerts upward pressure on the workpiece. That's two forces you must counteract to maintain control. Press down with your left hand while using your right hand, with the help of a push stick, to push the workpiece forward.

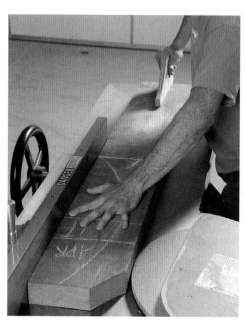

Keep pressure near the cutterhead. After the board is 6 in. to 12 in. past the cutterhead, let it pass under your left hand, but continue to apply downward pressure.

Drill press

Not as obviously dangerous as a tablesaw or bandsaw, the drill press can still ruin an otherwise fine day. When the spinning bit punches through the bottom of a workpiece, it can rip that piece from your hand, driving it into the column, or worse, your hand or body. Clamp the workpiece to the table or hold it against a fence to prevent the bit's force from spinning it out of control (see p. 88).

Router table

Always feed the workpiece against the bit's rotation. At the router table, this means it travels from right to left across the table. This counteracts the bit's rotational force, allowing you to control the workpiece. Because the bit also exerts force toward the back of the table, you should use a fence. The bit will push the workpiece against the fence, helping you to stabilize it during the cut.

Prevent spinning work on the drill-press table. A clamp with a deep throat adds stabilizing pressure next to the bit (top), and keeps the workpiece from spinning or lifting from the table as you back out the bit. A fence clamped to the drill-press table prevents it from spinning as well (above).

Two hands, one fence. No downward pressure is needed; use your left hand to press the workpiece against the fence. Your right hand feeds it through the cut, countering the force of the bit.

Drill-Press Cutting Force

At the drill press, the bit can spin the workpiece.

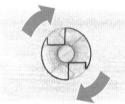

HOW TO CONTROL IT

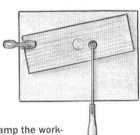

Clamp the workpiece to the table. This also prevents it from lifting when the bit backs out.

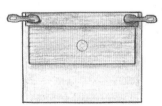

A fence attached to the table stops rotation, too.

Router-Table Cutting Forces

If fed from left to right, a board is pushed away from the fence and pulled away from you.

HOW TO CONTROL THEM

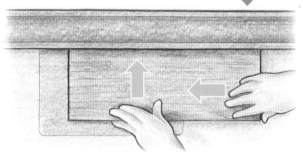

Instead, always feed from right to left, using your left hand like a featherboard to hold the workpiece against the fence in front of the bit while pushing it through with your right hand. For narrow pieces, use a push stick or a push pad.

Safe Ripping on the Tablesaw

BOB VAN DYKE

A tablesaw is the best tool for ripping a board's edges parallel, but safe and successful ripping on the tablesaw depends on understanding a handful of essential techniques and practices. Here, I will explore and explain these factors so that you can master the mechanics of ripping.

One important concept to keep in mind is the rotation of the blade. Think of the blade as having a front and a back, and remember that as they cut, the teeth in the front push the wood down onto the saw table. At the back, the teeth are rotating up away from the table, and if wood contacts these rising teeth, they'll exert upward pressure, creating the possibility of kickback. Kickback happens when the back of the blade contacts the edge of the wood with enough force that it grabs the stock and propels it back straight toward you at great speed. I once saw a piece of molding shoot 20 ft. across the shop before going completely through two pieces of ¾-in.-thick particleboard. Fortunately, as long as certain practices are followed, kickback is easy to avoid and should never be common.

Another important concept is that ripping requires more force than crosscutting. Picture the board's grain as a bundle of straws. Cutting across the bundle does not require as much force because once cut, the fibers don't exert pressure against the blade.

When ripping, however, the blade cuts lengthwise through the straws. Because the grain is not always straight, picture a bundle of bendy straws instead of straight ones. This irregularity, plus the fact that these fibers are usually under tension, means that as the fibers are cut, the tensions within the board change and it can push against the blade, thus requiring more force to cut through the wood. To overcome this, install a more aggressive blade for rips, one that has fewer teeth (24 is standard for a rip blade) and larger gullets.

Prep the stock. It is never a good idea to cut roughsawn wood on the tablesaw. Instead, turn to the bandsaw to rough cut stock for milling (left). Then, to avoid kickback from warped boards, joint the face that will ride on the saw table and the edge that will be against the fence (above).

Stock must be flat and straight

For safe, clean ripping, the face of the board that rides on the table and the edge riding the fence must be flat and straight. If they're not, the stock can easily move during the cut and kick back. Avoiding this is easy. Always use the bandsaw to break down roughsawn stock. And then joint the face that will be against the saw table and the edge that will be against the fence.

The adjustment of the saw's fence is also crucial. Never assume that a saw coming from the manufacturer is correctly adjusted, and be aware that all saws can go out of adjustment over time. The rip fence must be parallel to the blade or heeled out slightly at the back.

Essential equipment. The splitter or the riving knife (depending on the design of your saw) is the one critical safety device that should always be on the saw when ripping. Positioned directly behind the blade, it fits into the kerf and prevents the stock from drifting off the fence, which could result in kickback. It also prevents the kerf from closing up on the back of the blade—another common cause of kickback.

Install a splitter and rip blade. Because ripping requires more force than crosscutting, a blade with fewer teeth and larger gullets is typically used. Behind it should be a riving knife or splitter, a crucial piece of safety equipment that minimizes the chance of kickback when ripping.

Square the fence. Use a combination square to check that the rip fence is parallel to the miter slot, or heeled out slightly so the gap between the fence and the slot is no more than $\frac{1}{64}$ in. wider at the back than at the front. This assumes that the blade is parallel to the miter slot.

How to stand, hold, and push

There is only one correct way to stand to easily ensure the edge of the board remains against the fence at all times: close to the front of the saw and a little to the left of the blade. This makes it easier to support the board as it enters the cut and easier to hold the board against the fence the whole way through the cut. Standing a little to the left also keeps you clear of a potential kickback.

The left hand. The left hand pushes the board against the fence and down onto the saw table simultaneously. Position your left hand about 1 in. in front of the throat plate and keep it there until the cut is nearly finished. Never move your left hand beyond the front of the throat plate. When the end of the stock nears the plate, move your left hand to hold onto the left edge of the saw. Holding here gives you a very firm stance as you lean forward and move to the right to complete the cut with your right hand.

The right hand. At the start of the cut, cup the end of the stock with your right hand and push forward. When your fingers meet the rail, pivot the hand so your pinkie is on the fence, your next three fingers are holding

Ripping 101. Standing in the right place and positioning your hands correctly will keep your rips true and your body out of harm's way. Stand close to the front of the saw and a little to the left of the blade. This makes it easier to support the board as you begin the cut and easier to hold the board against the fence the whole way through. Because you are standing slightly to the left at this point, you won't be hit by a kickback, which typically goes straight back when ripping.

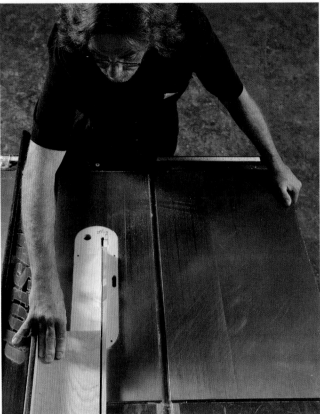

Hook a ride on the fence. When the fingers of your right hand hit the rail, pivot your hand around so your pinkie is hooked on the fence; your ring, middle, and index fingers are pushing the board down and slightly toward the fence (and so is your left hand); and your right thumb is on the end of the board midway between the blade and the fence.

Hand off. As the end of the stock approaches the throat plate, making the risk of kickback minimal, move your left hand to hold onto the left edge of the saw, giving you a firm stance as you push the board through the rest of the cut with your right hand. Unless the board is wider than 8 in., your right hand stays hooked on the fence. If it's wider, position your hand midway between the fence and blade. Do not release the board until it is completely past the blade and riving knife.

the board down and toward the fence, and your thumb is on the end. Do not release the board until it is past the riving knife. When ripping a board wider than 8 in., have the whole hand on the board to keep it against the fence.

Essential accessories

While your hands alone give you the most control when ripping, there are times when some accessories are crucial.

Push sticks. Push sticks keep your right hand safe when ripping narrow stock. Be mindful, though: While push sticks do a good job pushing, they can't exert as much lateral pressure toward the fence as your hand. To determine if a cut requires a push stick, simply make a fist. If your fist fits between the blade and the fence (be sure to turn off the saw before making this test!), use your hand. If not, pick up a push stick.

Before the cut, make sure the push stick is next to—not on top of—the fence so it's easy to grab. Never use a push stick while the end of the board is off the table, unsupported. Wait until the end of the stock is almost at the throat plate.

Shopmade Push Stick

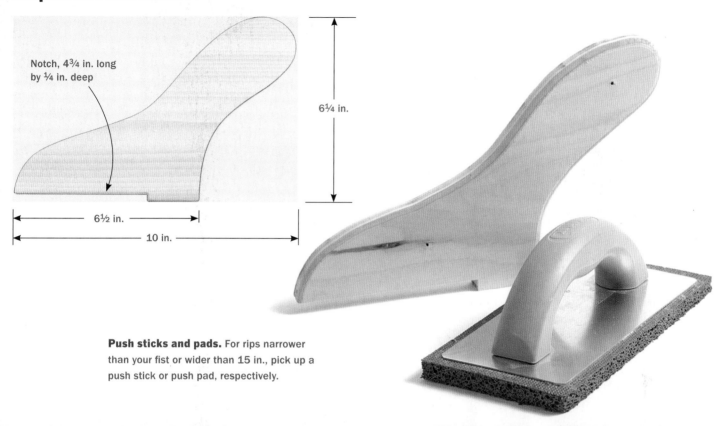

Notch, 4¾ in. long
by ¼ in. deep

6¼ in.

6½ in.

10 in.

Push sticks and pads. For rips narrower than your fist or wider than 15 in., pick up a push stick or push pad, respectively.

Push stick for narrow rips. Start the rip as you normally would (1). As the end of the board reaches the table, hold it in place with your left hand as you pick up the push stick (2). Remove your left hand and use the push stick to finish the cut while adding lateral pressure to keep the stock against the fence (3).

Grout float handles wide stock. When ripping wide stock, Van Dyke uses a grout float as a push pad. Unlike some push pads sold for woodworking, its spongy pad is very grippy and enables him to exert lateral and forward pressure. To make sure he can reach it when necessary, he places it on top of the stock before starting the rip.

I make my own push sticks out of scrap plywood (drawing, p. 93). These work better than the ones that come with saws, which are typically just a plastic stick with a small V at the end. And since my push sticks are made from scrap, I don't have to worry about cutting into them during narrow rips.

Featherboards. Featherboards are designed to take the place of the left hand. Positioned in front of the blade, they hold the stock against the fence.

Featherboards are helpful when making repetitive cuts and when cutting large or awkward pieces. For more information about them, see my article, "Work more safely with featherboards," in *Fine Woodworking* #224.

Special circumstances

Occasionally, the size or shape of the board being ripped will require you to change tactics.

If the board is too long to comfortably hold on the end, your right hand should hold its right edge until enough stock has gone through the blade that you can comfortably move your right hand to the end of the board. I also like to use a removable infeed support for ripping long stock (drawing, facing page, and photos, p. 96).

As a rule of thumb, if you have a wide piece that is shorter than the width of the blade projecting out of the saw table, rip it using a sled or miter gauge. It is unsafe to rip these

A Helping Hand for Long Stock

This removable infeed support, made from scrap, supports long stock so you can focus on ripping. Adapt the dimensions to your saw if necessary.

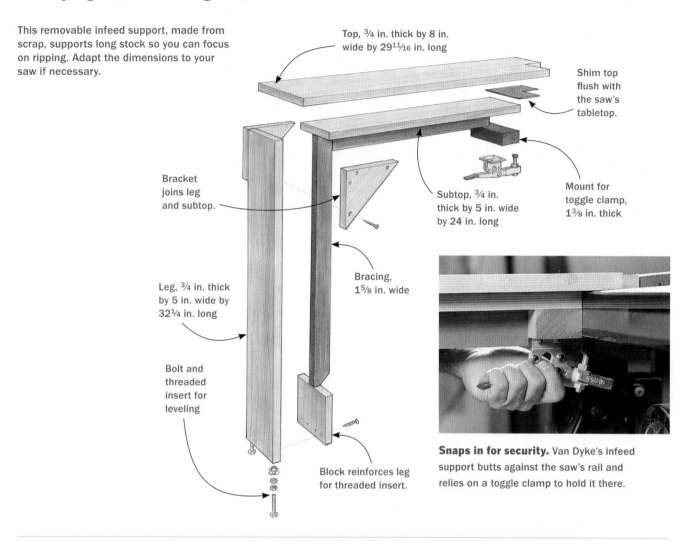

Top, ¾ in. thick by 8 in. wide by 29¹¹⁄₁₆ in. long

Shim top flush with the saw's tabletop.

Bracket joins leg and subtop.

Subtop, ¾ in. thick by 5 in. wide by 24 in. long

Mount for toggle clamp, 1³⁄₈ in. thick

Leg, ¾ in. thick by 5 in. wide by 32¼ in. long

Bracing, 1⅝ in. wide

Bolt and threaded insert for leveling

Block reinforces leg for threaded insert.

Snaps in for security. Van Dyke's infeed support butts against the saw's rail and relies on a toggle clamp to hold it there.

using the fence because the extra width will tend to drag the back edge of the board away from the fence and into the back of the blade.

Ripping plywood is usually a lot simpler than solid stock, as there is no grain direction to consider. Nevertheless, when ripping wide pieces of plywood, it's easy for the stock to come away from the fence—which can cause a kickback that acts differently. Rather than heading straight back, it will arc across the blade, putting your right hand in extreme danger. Luckily, the riving knife or splitter

prevents this situation. Also, a very effective aid for controlling wide plywood is a grout float. The spongy surface gives you a nonslip grip, making it a lot easier to hold the stock against the fence.

Ripping is a basic and necessary function on the tablesaw that requires your total respect and undivided attention. It should never cause paralyzing fear. If you simply understand that the board must stay against the table and rip fence, you will be on your way toward success.

Stable setup. Feeding long stock into a tablesaw can be difficult without the proper support, so Van Dyke uses a specially made infeed support (left) that holds his stock at the right height, leaving him one less thing to worry about. If a board is so long you can't comfortably reach your right hand back to the end, grip the right edge of the board (center) and push until enough stock has gone through the blade that you can comfortably move your hand to the end of the board. Then the rip proceeds like any other (right).

3 Handy Stop Blocks

BOB VAN DYKE

We've all heard the old adage "Measure twice, cut once," but when it comes to cutting parts to length on the tablesaw, it's better to measure once, then use a stop block. Stops ensure that identical parts end up at identical lengths and that corresponding joinery ends up in the right spots. Instead of measuring individual parts, you measure once to locate the stop block and then use the block as a registration point when cutting the parts to size.

I use three stops pretty much every day at the tablesaw. The one that gets the heaviest use is a flip stop made from two blocks of wood and a quality butt hinge. It's perfect for cutting multiple parts to final length. For tenons and notches, I use an adjustable stop made from a block of wood with a screw in the end. It's great because you can turn the screw to make fine adjustments to the stop. The third stop, which I picked up from my friend, *Fine Woodworking* contributing editor Steve Latta, is a two-part stop. It has a sliding arm that can be pulled out of the way before you make the cut. It's ideal for cutting anything less than 3 in. long.

I'll show you how to set up and use these blocks. They're so simple to make and use, you'll find yourself reaching for them all the time, and you'll see an improvement in the accuracy of your work as a result.

FLIP STOP

SCREW STOP

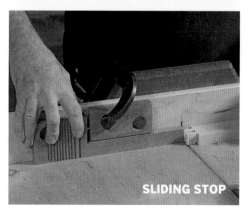

SLIDING STOP

Flip stop is the perfect crosscut companion

My favorite stop is the flip stop, which I first saw years ago in a *Fine Woodworking* article by Tage Frid. It works so well because you can clamp it to a sled's fence or to a miter gauge and both square the first end and cut the part to length without the stop getting in the way. First you set the stop to cut the part to length. Then simply slide the part under the stop and make the first squaring cut. Pull the part out, let the stop flip down, and then put the square end against the stop to cut it to length.

There are two advantages to the flip stop that make it way better than a simple block of wood clamped to the fence. First, because the stop swings above the surface, sawdust won't build up between it and the workpiece. Also, because the first cut is made with the workpiece slid under the flip section, it is impossible to cut the part too short. With a block clamped to the fence, you are forced to square the first end holding the workpiece on the opposite side of the sled and then to slide the squared end down to the stop. Trust me, with that technique, it's easy to cut the part too short when squaring the first end.

I use the flip stop every day in my shop, and I often use two at once so that I can cut more than one part to length without moving the stop.

(continued on p. 102)

Flip Stop

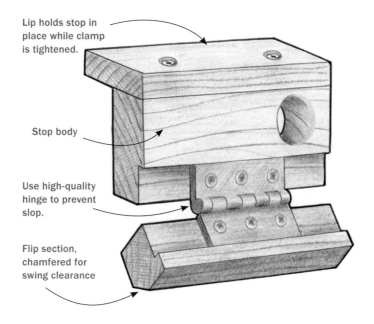

Lip holds stop in place while clamp is tightened.

Stop body

Use high-quality hinge to prevent slop.

Flip section, chamfered for swing clearance

Measure from the kerf. For this to work, the kerf must be zero-clearance. To set the length of cut, Van Dyke props up the rule so that it's high enough to butt against the stop's swinging block.

Go under the stop to square one end. As long as the workpiece is even a hair under the stop, you know that you're not cutting it too short.

Drop the stop. Set the freshly cut square end against the swinging block and cut the part to length. For a second part the same length, slide the offcut down to the stop and cut again.

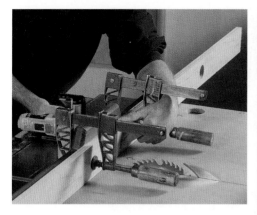

Long parts need a long fence. Some furniture parts, such as aprons or legs, can be quite long, and the everyday fence on your sled might be too short to clamp on a stop. The solution? Screw a longer fence to the sled so that you can still use a flip stop.

Two stops are better than one. When you need to make multiples of more than one part—such as the rails and stiles for a set of cabinet doors—you'll get through the cuts more quickly and accurately if you use two stops instead of moving one stop. Use one for the longer part and another for the shorter one.

Go under to get around. Because the flip section of the stop swings up and out of the way, you can slide long workpieces under it to make use of a second stop. This allows you to cut multiple parts to length without having to move a stop.

Screw Stop

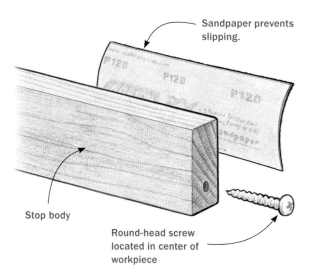

Sandpaper prevents slipping.

Stop body

Round-head screw located in center of workpiece

Pinpoint accuracy with an adjustable screw stop

You can make any stop block micro-adjustable simply by driving a screw into the end of the block. The screw adds amazing precision when cutting joinery like tenon shoulders. Use a round-head screw so that there is a single point of contact, even if the screw isn't driven in straight. It should be about ⅜ in. above the block's bottom edge, creating a space for sawdust. Without the screw, sawdust tends to get trapped between the stop and the workpiece. And because you can drive the screw farther in and back it out, you can easily dial in the stop without unclamping it from the fence.

The exact location of the screw is usually not important, but I try to install it so that the crown of the head is near the center of the workpiece's thickness. Also, I attach some sandpaper to the back of the stop to prevent it from slipping when clamping it to the fence. And the best way to adjust the screw is with a small ratcheting driver equipped with a screw bit.

This is a tremendously versatile and accurate stop. Through the years, I've accumulated a box of them, and I think you will, too.

Get in the ballpark. After aligning a layout line on the workpiece with the sled's zero-clearance kerf, Van Dyke clamps the stop to the fence. The screw's head is against the end of the workpiece.

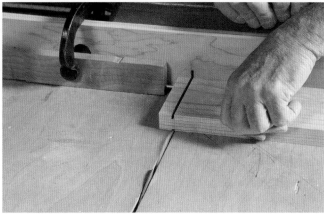

Adjust and cut. Make a test cut to check the stop's placement, then turn the screw in or out as needed to bring the workpiece's layout line in perfect alignment with the blade (left). Set the part against the screw and make the cut. Here, Van Dyke is cutting a tenon shoulder (right).

Double up for notches. Setting stops precisely to cut the two ends of a notch can be tough, but the small adjustments afforded by the screw make the job much easier.

A stop for small parts

I use this sliding stop to cut parts that are too short to cut safely with any standard stop. Very short pieces can't be held safely between the stop and blade, but if they can't be held securely, you run the risk of kickback. This stop overcomes that problem because it slides out of the way after it locates and registers the workpiece in the correct location for the cut. It's perfect for trimming a small amount from a workpiece, like when shortening a tenon, where the offcut would get caught between the blade and a standard stop.

There are two parts to this stop (see the drawing on p. 104). The fixed stop, which is a variation on the adjustable screw stop, is clamped to the sled's fence with the screw on the back end. The sliding stop is shaped like an L. The long leg slides under the fixed stop. It extends out past the stop, toward the blade. The short leg stands up and hits the screw head.

Sliding Stop

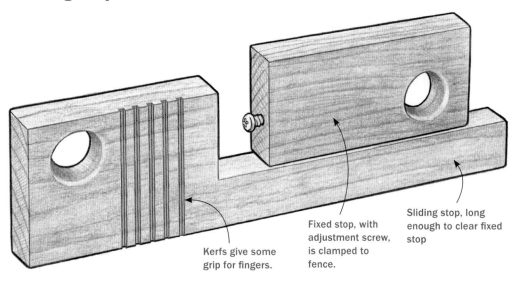

Kerfs give some grip for fingers.

Fixed stop, with adjustment screw, is clamped to fence.

Sliding stop, long enough to clear fixed stop

Using a sliding stop. Start by clamping the fixed stop to the fence. Place a rule or other removable spacer between the fixed stop and sliding stop to create a space that lets you move the sliding stop in and out smoothly (1). The screw on the block allows fine adjustments. To make a cut, bring the sliding stop against the fixed stop and push the workpiece against it (2). Then pull back the sliding stop holding the workpiece in place with the opposite hand (3). Because the offcut isn't trapped between the blade and stop, it won't get thrown by the blade during the cut (4).

Simple Box-Joint Sled

DOUG STOWE

Box joints, also called finger joints, are incredibly strong thanks to all their long-grain glue surface interlocking finger by finger. But these joints have distinct advantages beyond strength. Once you have a jig set up, they are quite quick to make. And the pattern of end grain vs. side grain at the corners creates a pleasing visual rhythm. The joint also can be scaled up, as in some Greene and Greene pieces. Luckily, finger joints offer all this while being very easy to cut.

Soup up a crosscut sled

While you can make box joints using a jig clamped to the miter gauge of your tablesaw, a dedicated sled is the better choice. Because it has two runners instead of the gauge's one, it provides a more stable and reliable platform.

A standard combination blade will work, but if using a single blade, I prefer rip blades because of their flat top, which leaves a cleaner joint than a combo blade's alternate top bevel. Similarly, for fingers wider than a standard sawblade's 1/8-in. kerf, you can use a regular dado stack, but I like box-joint blade sets, which come with a pair of blades that leave a flat-topped kerf in two fixed widths. Alternatively, you can send a typical dado stack to a saw sharpener to have the teeth ground flat on top.

Start by building a small crosscut sled, making sure the fence is square to the blade. Clamp a board to its fence and cut a kerf in it. Remove the board and fit a hardwood pin into the kerf. A tight fit is best. Glue the pin in place.

Before you clamp the pin board back into place against the fence, grab an offcut from the pin stock. Because the pin's width matches the kerf—and the fingers—this will help you zero in on the joint spacing. Push the offcut against the side of the sawblade, and slide the pin board over until the pin abuts the offcut. Clamp the pin board here.

Box-Joint Sled

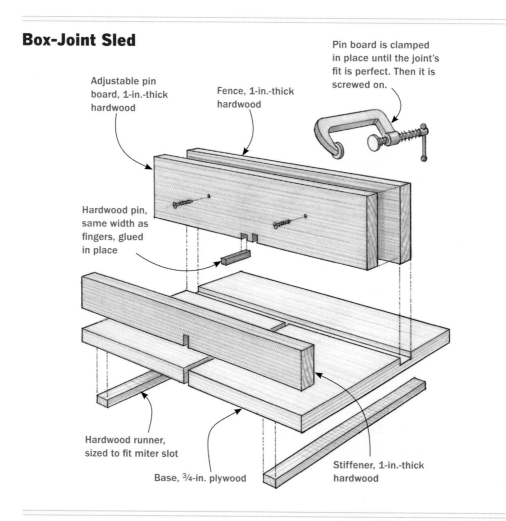

Adjustable pin board, 1-in.-thick hardwood

Fence, 1-in.-thick hardwood

Pin board is clamped in place until the joint's fit is perfect. Then it is screwed on.

Hardwood pin, same width as fingers, glued in place

Hardwood runner, sized to fit miter slot

Base, 3/4-in. plywood

Stiffener, 1-in.-thick hardwood

Make the jig. With the adjustable pin board clamped to the fence of a crosscut sled, saw a kerf through it. Stowe fits scrapwood stops into his miter slots to limit the jig's travel so he doesn't expose too much of the blade at the end of the cut.

Fit the pin. Remove the pin board and fit a hardwood pin into the kerf. You want a friction fit. Glue the pin to keep it stable.

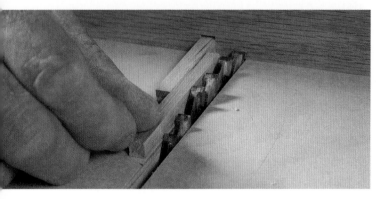

Offcut approximates spacing. While you'll fine-tune the fit later, placing an offcut from the pin stock between the pin and blade will get you pretty close.

TIP For box joints wider than the standard ⅛-in. kerf, you can use a specialty box-joint blade set. These cut a flat-topped kerf and work by stacking two blades, either inside to inside or outside to outside, for a pair of fixed widths.

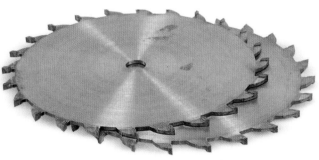

Clamps for now. For your test cuts, the pin board should be clamped to the sled's fence, allowing you to hold things temporarily in position as you home in on a perfect fit for the fingers.

How to get the fit just right.
Cut fingers on two pieces of
scrap stock. Straddle the pin
securely. Clear any dust that
collects, since it can throw off
your accuracy.

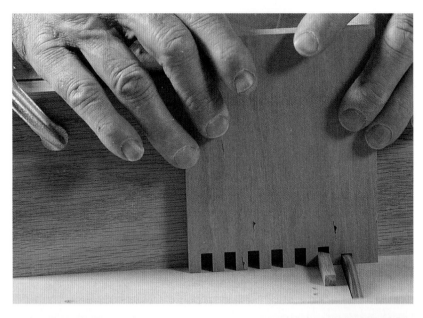

Too tight. You shouldn't have to force the parts together. To open
up the joint, slide the pin toward the blade.

Just right. A perfect fit is when the parts slide together without
being forced or hammered.

Dial in the fit

I advise making a run of fingers on two scrap
boards to dial in the spacing and make sure
the final fit is consistently tight. Align one
corner of a board against the pin and make
the first cut. Then fit that first notch over
the pin to make the second cut. Continue
walking the fingers over until you've
finished that edge. Repeat these steps on a
second board.

Too loose. Since this joint relies on glue, avoid visible gaps. The
fingers are too loose if you pick up two joined pieces and one falls
off. To close the gaps, slide the pin away from the blade.

Aim for a friction fit. It's good to have a bit of room for glue, but avoid visible gaps. If you need to tighten the joint, loosen the clamps and tap the pin board so the pin moves away from the blade; to loosen the fit, tap the pin board in the opposite direction. When the joint is just right, screw the pin board in place. As long as you're making boxes with the same joint spacing and using the same blade (or combination of blades), you won't need to readjust the jig.

Making boxes

Compared with making two test boards, building a four-sided box with box joints requires only a few extra, albeit important, steps. First, set the sawblade's height a little higher than the thickness of the stock so the fingers can be sanded flush later. Push the workpiece against the pin to create a full finger with the first cut. Then cut fingers across the rest of the board. The next part is crucial: To cut the fingers on the other end, flip the stock over end for end. If you don't, the joints will not align. Do this for a pair

of parts, either the front and back or the two sides.

Whichever pair you tackle second, you'll approach differently, making the first cuts while using an already-cut piece as a spacer. For this, take a just-cut piece and place the first finger between the pin and blade. Slide an uncut piece up to it and make the first cut. This offsets the mating fingers, allowing the two boards to interlock. To keep track of which parts need to start with a spacer, I cut the initial notches for all four ends that require the spacer, then remove the spacer and form the rest of the fingers.

I prefer to cut the fingers while the stock is slightly overwidth, and I trim to width only after I know exactly where the final finger falls. This lets me deal with any error that may creep in. For instance, when making a box with $\frac{1}{4}$-in. fingers, one would expect the dimensions to fall at some exact $\frac{1}{4}$-in. increment, but they often do not. If the $\frac{1}{4}$-in. finger fits best in a slot that's an extra $\frac{1}{64}$ in. wide, over the course of 5 in., that would add slightly more than $\frac{1}{16}$ in.

Screws set the fence. When you've established the perfect fit, screw the pin board in place. This jig will now work with any box you make using this blade.

Offcut sets the blade height. Raise the blade about $\frac{1}{64}$ in. above the stock to create a cleanup allowance. The fingers can be sanded flush to the box sides following assembly.

First set. Align one corner of a board against the pin and make the first cut.

The pin registers the cuts. Complete the kerfs across the end of the board. Stowe starts with the front and back boards.

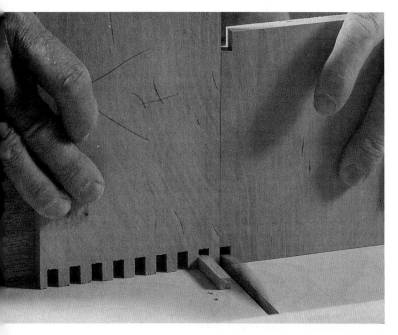

Second set needs a spacer. For the first cuts on the second pair of boards, use an already-cut piece as a spacer. Put its first kerf over the pin and slide an end up to it. Stowe cuts the first notches on each end of both boards before removing the spacer.

Finish the fingers. Remove the spacer and complete the remaining cuts.

For all your cuts, make sure the parts are nested carefully over the pin. If the stock isn't placed accurately and held down throughout the cut, the box sides won't come together correctly.

To install a bottom, I use a router table and a ⅛-in. bit to run a groove. I generally locate the groove ⅛ in. from the lower edge when using ⅛-in. Baltic-birch plywood for the bottom. Two of the parts will have a finger at the bottom edge, and they get stopped grooves; the other two parts get through-grooves.

One great thing about a box with well-cut box joints is that clamps are often unnecessary. But keep some handy just in case a corner needs persuasion. If it does, be sure to clamp close to the joints and not at the middle of the box, where the pressure will flex and distort the sides.

Groove for the bottom. To prepare for a bottom panel, Stowe routs ⅛ in. above the lower edge. Two parts get a stopped groove, two get a through-groove.

Trim the excess. Stowe cuts the fingers in stock that is a little wide and rips it to width later. This lets him clean up any cumulative error, like the thin finger on the right, that may have crept in.

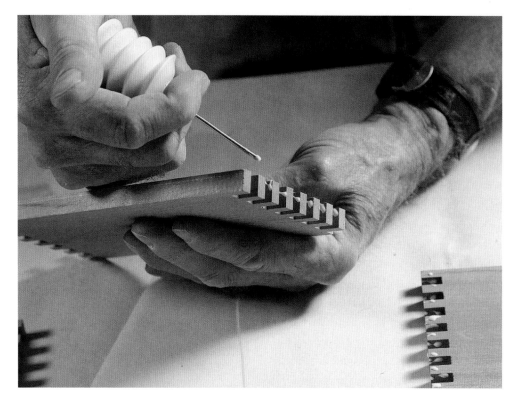

Glue the fingers. Apply a drop of glue to the edges where the parts slide together. The glue will spread as the fingers interlock.

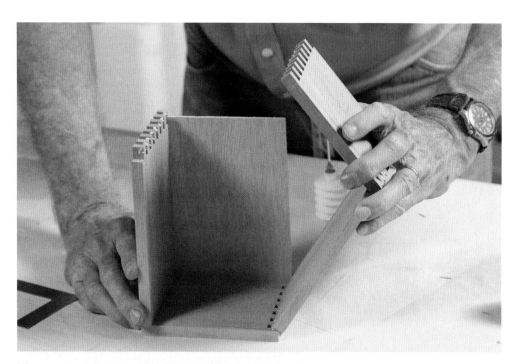

Wrap up. Assemble the sides around the bottom. If the parts are cut well, clamps may not be needed. Friction is often enough to hold the pieces. Check for square before letting the glue set.

Tablesaw Sled for Miters

CRAIG THIBODEAU

Frame miters—used to make doors, face frames, and picture frames—look easy but are deceptively difficult to do cleanly and without gaps. Not only do the parts need to be cut at exactly 45° (and any inaccuracy is compounded in the two halves of each joint), but the parts also need to be cut to the correct length. Even if you cut the parts and miters right, you still have the challenge of getting the angled surfaces clamped and glued properly.

I use frame miters quite often in my contemporary-style work, most frequently on the tops of tables and cabinets, where the frame surrounds and protects a veneered panel. Through experience, I've developed some surefire methods for cutting and clamping these joints.

The key to my success is twofold. First, I use a dedicated miter sled for the tablesaw. Second, I cut the parts to final length at 90° first, then I use the fresh-cut ends as the reference for the actual miter cuts done on the sled. This method helps me cut miters precisely the first time, without a lot of test-fitting and recutting.

Dedicated to Miters

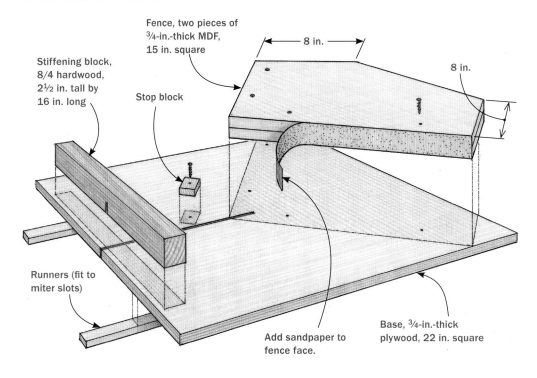

Fence, two pieces of ¾-in.-thick MDF, 15 in. square

Stiffening block, 8/4 hardwood, 2½ in. tall by 16 in. long

Stop block

8 in.

8 in.

Runners (fit to miter slots)

Add sandpaper to fence face.

Base, ¾-in.-thick plywood, 22 in. square

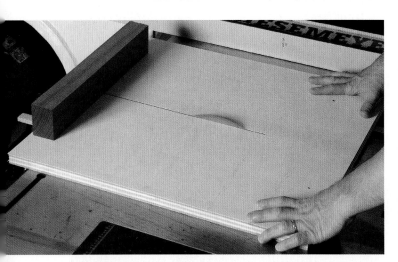

The sled is easy to make. After attaching a stiffening block to the front of the base and installing runners, cut a kerf in the base, stopping the cut a little more than halfway through.

Add a guide line. Use a drafting triangle to draw a perfect 45° line to set up the fence. Align the edge of the triangle with the left edge of the sawkerf.

Install the fence. Align it with the 45° line and screw it down on one side.

Get a grip. Glue a thin strip of 100-grit sandpaper to the fence face.

Sled guarantees a perfect joint

My miter sled cuts both left- and right-hand miters easily and accurately. It's essentially a standard crosscut sled, but I add a 45° fence to it.

Once you have the runners and stiffening block on your sled, make a stopped cut down the center of the sled base. Then mark a 45° line on one side of the kerf, using a 45° drafting square placed against the sawkerf. You'll use this line to adjust the fence at roughly 45°. Screw down one side of the fence, then make some test cuts using frame offcuts. Cut all of the mitered pieces on one side of the sled only. That way when you put them together, the error is doubled. If you were to cut one piece on each side of the sled, the corner would end up 90°, but one side might be 47° and the other 43°. The test pieces and all the frame pieces you make must be flat, straight, and square.

Dial in the fence. Test-cut miters on the ends of two frame pieces using the same fence face (top), then check the fit around a machinist's square (above).

Adjust the fence as needed. If the test miters show a gap, it should be small. The solution is to give the fence a light tap on the edge to move it left or right. Then make another round of test cuts. Keep adjusting until you no longer have a gap.

Fix a Gap

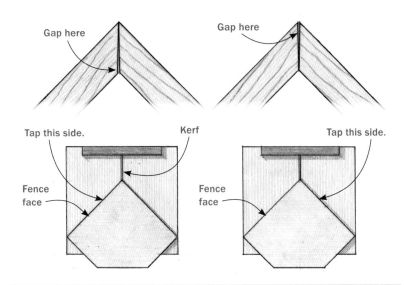

Gap here

Gap here

Tap this side. Kerf Tap this side.

Fence face Fence face

Lock it down. Once the jig is making perfect miter cuts, screw down the fence on both sides of the kerf. Clamp the fence down tightly while you do this.

Your first test cuts should be very close to 45°. Once they are exactly 45°, clamp and screw down the opposite side of the fence. Be sure to locate the screws so they will not be in the path of the blade. Then cut another set of miters and check to make sure they are perfect. If they are not, loosen the screws slightly and give the fence a light tap with a mallet to adjust it in the correct direction.

Stop block ensures success

When the sled is finished and cutting perfectly, you're ready to cut some miters. As I mentioned, I cut the parts to length before mitering them. This enables me to use an unusual stop-block setup that ensures accuracy and keeps me from ever having to use the point of a miter for measurement or reference. The key to the setup is that the stop block is placed on the cutoff side of the blade. I locate the block by placing one frame piece on the sled with the forward corner aligned with the edge of the sawkerf. Then I place the stop block flush with the end and screw it in place. The stop block can then be used to index all of the frame parts by cutting them all on one side of the sled and it will cut them all the same. You'll have to change out the block for different-size frame pieces.

I use a standard combination blade for these cuts and they come out very clean with no tearout, because the bottom of the crosscut sled is essentially a zero-clearance surface. Try to push the sled from the center so that you're not favoring one side or the other while cutting. If you've taken the time necessary to get the sled aligned perfectly, there is no need for additional adjustment of any of the miter joints on a disk sander or other tool.

The secret to success. Cut all the frame parts to final length. Use a stop block for accuracy and a backer to prevent blowout.

Add a stop block. With a frame piece against the fence, align its forward corner with the left edge of the sawkerf and position a stop block against its end. Clamp the frame piece in place and screw down the block (above and right).

Stop-Block Setup

Kerf

Stop block

Fence

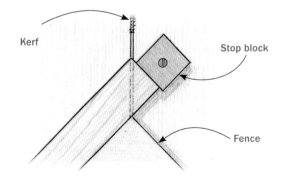

Happy mitering. With the parts cut to final length, all you have to do is align them with the stop block, add a clamp, and cut. The offcuts simply fall away, leaving perfect miters behind.

Clever Clamping Tricks Ease Assembly

When it comes to gluing miters, there are two big issues. First, this is a weak end-grain joint, so you have to take extra steps to ensure a good bond. Because the end grain will soak up glue quickly, I recommend double-coating the joint. Apply glue to all the end-grain parts, wait a few minutes until the first application of glue has soaked into the end grain, and then coat them all again before assembly.

To ensure a long, gap-free life, I reinforce miters with Domino slip tenons (biscuits and splines work, too). The Dominos also keep parts aligned while clamping, reducing the need for sanding or planing later.

The next challenge with miters is applying pressure at 90° to the mitered surfaces and in the center of the joint. To help, I use the small triangular offcuts from the mitering process as clamping cauls. Sometimes I glue them to thin ¼-in. MDF strips. I clamp a pair of these at each corner of the frame during glue-up. These work very well for picture frames, but I take a different approach for situations where it's not convenient to clamp them to a frame from the inside, such as a frame-and-panel assembly. In these cases, I just glue the offcuts to the frame pieces and then bandsaw and plane them off after assembly.

When I have a frame with molded edges, I make cauls that are roughly the reverse of the molding profile. They don't need to be exact, but they should make enough contact to be glued securely in place. Once the caul is shaped, glue it in place with a bit of yellow glue, making sure the clamping surface lines up with the miter. After the frame is assembled, these blocks will be cut off using a bandsaw or handsaw. Then the frame gets planed and sanded smooth.

Clamped-on cauls for flat frames. To prevent the parts from sliding out of alignment, Thibodeau uses slip tenons inside and clamped-on cauls on the outside. The tenons add strength, too. The cauls are made by gluing the miter offcuts to strips of MDF.

Pressure where you need it. When clamping on the cauls, align the corner blocks so that clamping pressure is centered across the joints (drawing, facing page).

Clamped-on Cauls

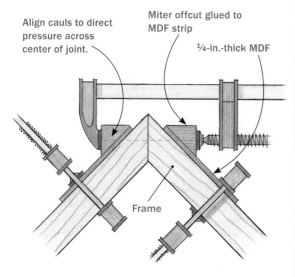

Align cauls to direct pressure across center of joint.

Miter offcut glued to MDF strip

¼-in.-thick MDF

Frame

The final step. Even with a tenon in the middle, parts can slip slightly. To lock them flush, use waxed cauls above and below the joints.

Glued-on cauls for frame-and-panel assemblies. In situations where the clamped-on cauls won't work, such as door panels, Thibodeau glues the miter offcuts to the frame parts. He glues the cauls in place with yellow glue and a rub joint.

Good pressure in the right spot. Position the cauls so that you get clamping pressure across the center of the joint.

(continued on p. 120)

Cut them off when you're done. After the glue dries on the assembly, cut off the cauls just proud of the frame edge, then plane the area flat.

Solution for shapely frames. To handle frames with complex shapes, Thibodeau fashions mirror-image cauls to fit the profile (above). He glues them to the frame to get solid pressure across the center of the joint (right). The cauls have to be cut off after the glue-up, and then the frame is planed, scraped, and sanded.

Add Muscle to Your Miters

DUNCAN GOWDY, TIMOTHY COLEMAN, AND REED HANSULD

For those who like their joinery subtle and seamless, the miter is indispensable. It allows long grain to flow around a door frame, over the edge of a case piece, or from leg to rail in a chair, unbroken by end grain. And it lets you join sheet goods without exposing the inner layers.

But the miter's glue surface—especially in solid wood—is mediocre, and the space for reinforcement, whether with biscuits, slip tenons, or splines, is limited and also compromised in terms of glue surface. For some years now, we've been seeing a clever solution used by a number of craftsmen: L-tenons, shopmade right-angle slip tenons that allow you to sink a long leg with plenty of face-grain glue surface into each member of a miter joint. L-tenons can be used with almost any sort of miter and on any scale.

We've brought together three fine makers who use the joint frequently, each taking a different approach but all ending up with what one calls "an indestructible miter joint."

Three Versions of the L-Tenon

Reinforcing miter joints with L-shaped tenons makes a beautiful joint suddenly much stronger. The tenons' 90° turn produces a joint with much more available glue surface, all of it face-grain. It also can make for simpler assembly.

Duncan Gowdy
Holden, Mass.

Box-jointed L-tenons

BOX-JOINTED IN SOLID WOOD

LAMINATED WOOD AND ALUMINUM

PLYWOOD

Flowing frame. With the powerful tenons hidden, Gowdy's mitered case works as a clean, elegant border for his carved doors.

Box-jointed L-tenons

Solid-wood cases with mitered corners are at the heart of my furniture making. Most of my pieces involve carving, and in pursuit of good surfaces to carve, I build wall cabinets, freestanding case pieces, and small boxes, most of them mitered. And on all of those miters I use L-tenons made by box-jointing two pieces of solid wood. Yes, I spend a fair amount of time making the tenons, but the resulting strength of the joint is well worth it. Using this technique, I've made L-tenons in sizes ranging from 3 in. across for large case pieces to barely ¾ in. for small boxes. The L-tenon miter joint allows for more straightforward assembly than typical splined miter joints, which must be assembled on the diagonal, often causing a bit of juggling in the glue-up.

Cut the joint. Gowdy cuts the mortises first with a horizontal mortiser, then uses a sled to cut the miters on a tablesaw.

Fit the strip. After making long blanks and rounding their edges with a bullnose bit on the router table, Gowdy fits them to the mortise.

Box-joint jig. Gowdy uses a dado blade and a dedicated tablesaw jig to cut the fingers. He cuts fingers on the first leg of a pair (above), then uses it as a spacer to make the first pass on the second leg (right).

Perfect 90. During glue-up, a drafting triangle held against the inside of the legs creates a reliable right angle. Once the glue has dried, Gowdy trims the proud fingers flush on the router table.

Glue slot. One careful pass over a tablesaw blade raised $\frac{1}{16}$ in. produces an escape route for glue.

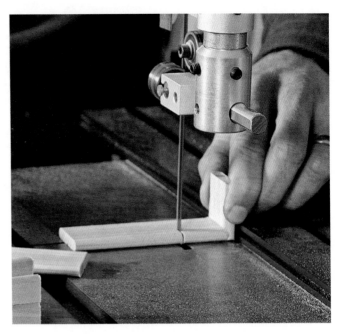

Off with the excess. A low fence at the bandsaw simplifies trimming the legs of the tenons to final length.

Quick chamfer. Break the edges with a few strokes of a sanding block.

Assemble the joint. With the opposite end of the case dry-fitted and clamped, Gowdy glues the tenons (above) and hammers the joint home (right). He achieves final tightness with quick-release clamps on the angled glue blocks.

Wood-and-aluminum L-tenons

Miters reinforced with L-tenons are very useful in casework and furniture, and I've experimented with several methods to create the tenons. I tried using solid wood, either finger-jointed or dovetailed, and I tried plywood. Then I discovered that by gluing strips of wood to aluminum angle stock, I could make strong L-tenons quickly.

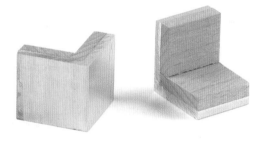

Wood-and-aluminum L-tenons

Timothy Coleman
Shelburne, Mass.

Strong and seamless. Coleman's veneered sideboard has mitered corners stocked with L-tenons.

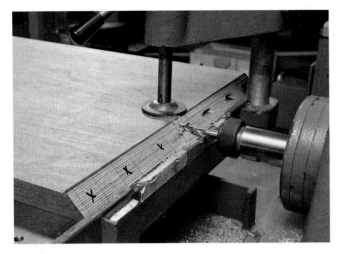

Cut the joint. Coleman cuts his miters first, then cuts the mortises with a horizontal mortiser. A router or Domino would work as well.

Clamp the sandwich. With the aluminum angle resting in a cradle and the wood strips glued, Coleman uses a square-section caul to distribute clamping pressure. The caul and the cradle are both waxed to resist glue.

I buy the aluminum angle at the hardware store in 3-ft.-long pieces that measure 1 in. on each side and ⅛ in. thick. It is accurately machined and extremely strong. By laminating strips of wood to the inside of the angle with polyurethane glue, I produce the blanks from which I cut individual tenons. The wood strip allows me to trim the thickness to match the mortise or slot in the miter. I use either the chopsaw or tablesaw to cut the tenons to width. For final assembly of the joint I typically use Titebond. I figure that the tenon will have wood-to-wood glue surfaces on one side, and the faces of the miter offer plenty of additional glue surface. For extra insurance, you could do the final glue-up with epoxy or polyurethane glue.

Chop chop. A regular woodworking blade in the chopsaw (or tablesaw) makes quick work of cutting the long blank into dozens of tenons.

Tenon trimming. Coleman trims the tenon to exact thickness by shaving the wood face on the bandsaw.

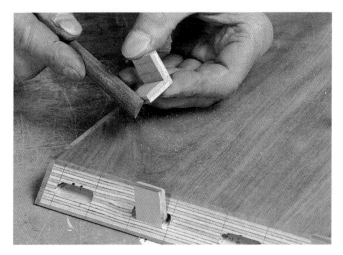

Chamfer if you must. A few strokes with a file ease the edges of the tenons. To avoid having to round over the side edges of the tenon, Coleman makes the mortises extra wide.

Two-step glue-up assembly. Coleman glues his tenons into one side of the case (left) and lets them dry, then glues them into the second side (above). This means that to close the joint he needs clamping pressure in only one direction.

Plywood L-tenons

I learned the L-shaped plywood tenon from David Upfill-Brown when he was teaching at the Center for Furniture Craftsmanship in Maine. He referred to it as "the indestructible miter joint." I haven't taken a sledgehammer to one of these joints, but since the technique utilizes deep tenons with face-grain glue surfaces combined with the stability and strength of plywood, David may well be right. I find these joints great for mitered casework both in solid wood and sheet goods, as well as for mitered frames and furniture. They can also be used where parts meet at angles other than 90°, and even for compound angles.

Reed Hansuld
Brooklyn, N.Y.

I make the tenons from Baltic-birch plywood, which is free of voids, and I cut the mortises with a Domino or a router. I produce the tenons by gluing up a long blank of plywood blocks and then slicing it up like a loaf of bread, which makes it easy to produce lots of identical tenons.

Plywood L-tenons

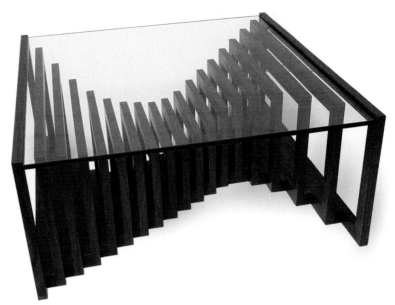

Frame job. Hansuld's coffee table has 19 mitered frames, each one reinforced with plywood L-tenons.

Miters after mortises. After using a Domino to cut the mortises on his frame members, Hansuld cuts the miters with a chopsaw.

Glue up a stacked blank. When gluing up the stack of Baltic-birch squares, be sure the grain direction on the face alternates in adjacent blocks. Hansuld marks each block to show grain direction. He uses cauls along all four sides of the stack to maintain alignment during the glue-up.

Rip to make a notch. First saw all four edges to create a clean, square blank. Then make two ripcuts with the blade at about half height to yield the L-shaped blank.

Slice off the tenons. Hansuld uses the miter gauge, with a stop block clamped to the fence to control thickness.

Notch the elbow. A side-to-side scrape at the bandsaw cuts a shallow notch that prevents the tenon from catching on the edge of the mortise during assembly.

Rout a radius on the edges. Working carefully and using a push block, Hansuld rounds over the edges of the tenon on the router table.

Final fit. To tweak the final fit, Hansuld rubs the tenons on 100-grit sandpaper adhered to plywood.

Assemble the frame. Hansuld glues all four joints at once, then applies pressure with quick-release clamps along the length and across the width of the frame.

When the Miters Aren't Square

Hansuld's bar stool is made with a series of mitered frames, none of them meeting at 90°. He made plywood tenons to reinforce all of them.

Bandsaw the notch. After gluing up a long blank and then cutting it to shape on the tablesaw, Hansuld creates the notch at the bandsaw.

Steady slicer. Using the notch cutoff as a push block, Hansuld slices the block into wide-angled tenons.

Screwy glue-up. With no easy purchase for clamps, Hansuld glues on angled clamping blocks. For compound angled joints, you can use wider mortises to allow some adjustment.

Shoulder Your Dovetails

STEVE LATTA

I can't remember when I started shouldering my dovetails, but it has been a regular practice for most of my years as a cabinetmaker. In my early days, I noticed the old-timers shouldered the dovetails on spice chests to avoid cutting half-blinds. They quickly cut through-dovetails and covered the joinery with a molding. This combined efficiency with cleanliness, and in my book that is always a winning combination. I've expanded the practice to just about all my dovetails. The lip allows for an easier, more positive registration and covers up any inaccuracies or slight chipping that may occur.

I'll walk you through my typical approach for drawer construction, the top stretcher of a table, and carcases. The order of operations is almost the same for all. It is easy and saves time while adding to the overall clean look of the piece.

Drawers with no twist

While creating the shoulder on a dovetailed drawer makes a huge difference to the stability and appearance of the finished product, shouldered dovetails aren't much more work to create.

After you fit the drawer front to the opening, lay out and cut the dovetails on the sides. I cut mine on the tablesaw using a customized blade for cutting dovetails. All the teeth are ground at 10° in one direction, and I tilt the sawblade 10° so its tip is parallel

131

to the saw table. I use a scrollsaw to remove the waste between tails.

I shoulder the tails on the tablesaw with a rip blade. Hold each drawer side on end against the fence to skim off about $1/16$ in. or so of material to create the shoulder. Now move on to the pins. Set a marking gauge to the thickness of the tails, and transfer them to the drawer front. Mark one side of the tails, wiggle the board to just cover those lines, and then mark the other side of the tails for a tight fit. With a handsaw, cut to the line on the sides, clear the sockets close to the line with a router, and pare to the lines with a chisel.

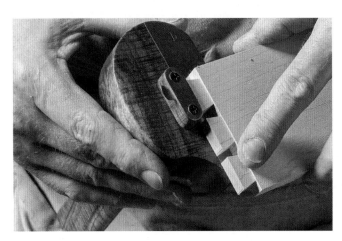

Cut the tails, create the shoulder, and mark the drawer front. Set a marking gauge to the thickness of the tails and score the drawer front (above). Then, registering on the shouldered tails, transfer them to the drawer front with a knife (right).

Flat and clean. The shoulders ensure square joinery and a drawer box that sits flat (left). They also conceal any gaps or sawcuts, leaving clean inside corners (above).

Creating the shoulder. Latta uses a miter gauge on the tablesaw to make the shoulder cuts on the faces and edges of the tail board. Using a test piece, creep up on the shoulder-to-shoulder distance until the shoulders exactly match those of the lower stretcher to ensure a square opening (above). Then, use a tenoning jig to make the cheek cut on each end of the upper rail (right).

Square drawer pockets in tables

Combining the shoulder with a double dovetail on the top stretcher not only makes transferring the layout easier, but it also ensures that the drawer pocket is dead-square. If the shoulder-to-shoulder distance of the bottom stretcher with double tenons matches the shoulder-to-shoulder distance of the top stretcher with the double dovetails and the back stretcher, the drawer box is guaranteed to be square. I typically use a double tail as opposed to a single one, because adding the second tail doubles the face-to-face glue surface.

In this situation, I use the tablesaw with a miter gauge to make the shoulder cuts for the tails. Then, with a tenoning jig, I make the cheek cut on each end of the upper rail.

Cut the tails. After establishing the shoulders, Latta cuts the tails on the scrollsaw, getting close to the layout lines, and then pares them clean with a chisel.

Transfer the tails to the top of the leg. Registering on the shoulder, score the ends of the tails on the top of the leg (left). For a tight fit, mark one side of the tails, move the board to just cover those lines, and then mark the other side. Rout the pin sockets, pare them with a chisel, and test the fit (above).

Square glue-ups and hidden joints in casework

Shouldering the dovetails on case pieces guarantees a square box, makes it easier to lay out the pins, and makes the tails easier to hide with molding. I cut the tails on the tablesaw, clean out the centers with a scrollsaw, and then pare them with a chisel. Then I use a router with a wooden fence clamped to it to cut the shoulder. The fence also creates a zero-clearance cavity that eliminates tearout. Once the shoulders are cut, transfer the tails to the pin boards.

Shouldered Dovetails

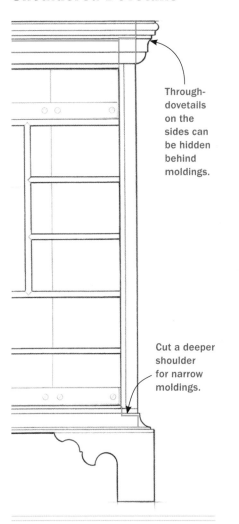

Through-dovetails on the sides can be hidden behind moldings.

Cut a deeper shoulder for narrow moldings.

Rout the shoulder and transfer the layout.
Latta cuts a deeper shoulder on the case bottom to make the tails thinner and easier to cover with the narrow molding. Clamping a wooden fence to the router makes it easy to cut the shoulders. Then, resting on the shoulders, transfer the tails to the pin board and cut the pins.

Thick Tabletops from Thin Stock

MARK EDMUNDSON

Whether it will stand in a stark modern house or in a rustic timber-frame, a table with a massive solid-wood top can be a powerful presence in a room. I often get requests for such tables, but here in Idaho there's no local supply of big hardwood trees, and getting 12/4 planks means ordering very expensive, very heavy slabs from far-off places, sight unseen, and paying for shipping. So once when a client asked for a 3-in.-thick tabletop it occurred to me I could make one from 4/4 solid stock. I could glue up an oversize panel, cut off strips along the sides and ends, and then miter those offcuts and fold them down to create the appearance of a solid slab.

After I glued up my first faux slab tabletop and cleaned the glue joints, a timber-framing buddy stopped by the shop. His first words were to ask me where I got the 12/4 black walnut for it. Even after examining the top, he didn't realize it was all 4/4. That's when I knew the faux version was a great alternative to the real thing.

To make the illusion even more convincing, I glue return strips inside the bottom of the edging, so if you grab the tabletop and feel underneath, it seems like a full-thickness slab. There was one hiccup, though. The first time I added those strips underneath, I noticed that the top of the table gave off a deep echo when thumped.

Mind Trick

You can use 4/4 boards to make what appears to be a solid slab top. Glue up an oversize panel, cut strips from all four sides, miter them, and reattach them as edging to give the top an apparent thickness of up to 4 in. Add a return underneath to complete the illusion.

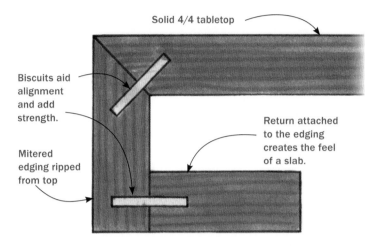

Solid 4/4 tabletop

Biscuits aid alignment and add strength.

Return attached to the edging creates the feel of a slab.

Mitered edging ripped from top

Bevel the Tabletop

Use a guided circular saw to miter all four edges of the oversize panel. The offcuts will become the edging and the return underneath.

1. Long edges first. With a sacrificial panel placed beneath the workpiece to support the offcuts, Edmundson uses a track saw with a long track to make smooth, accurate miter cuts along the length of the table. He's careful to ensure that the cuts on either side are parallel to each other.

2. Now square the ends. Square the track to the long miter cuts you've made, and then make the miter cuts across the width of the workpiece.

I solved that problem by adding a piece of ¾-in.-thick plywood to the underside. That deadened the noise completely. It also made the top easier to attach to the base, since I could screw the plywood to the base and then attach the solid top through slotted holes that accommodate seasonal movement.

If you choose not to add the return strips, you won't get the drum sound and you can forego the plywood. One other note: Using this technique, the miter where the side and end edging pieces meet is a cross-grain joint, so I wouldn't make one of these tabletops more than 4 in. thick.

No Track Saw? No Problem

You can use a good standard circular saw to cut clean miters by making a simple guide. Glue a fence to a plywood or MDF base, then tilt the sawblade to 45° and make a cut along the base to create a zero-clearance guide. Clamp the guide to the panel to make the miter cuts.

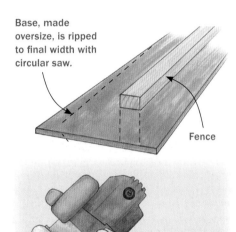

Base, made oversize, is ripped to final width with circular saw.

Fence

Clamp guide to workpiece.

Make the End Edging First

Trim and re-miter the cutoffs to make the end edging. At glue-up, ensure the face of the edging is square to the top surface; this simplifies adding the side edging.

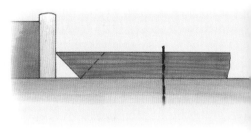

Rip one edge parallel. At the tablesaw, with the blade vertical, run the tip of the cutoff's miter against the fence and rip the other edge square. Cut close to final width, so you get a good-size offcut to use for the return.

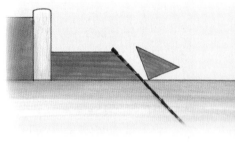

Recut the miter. Set the blade to 45° and cut a miter in the other direction. Because you're using offcuts from the panel, the ends of the edging are already properly mitered.

Offset the biscuit toward the bottom of the workpiece to prevent the slot from cutting through the surface.

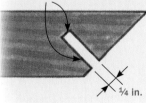

¼ in.

Biscuits reinforce the joints. Be sure to place a biscuit very close to the end of the joint to keep that area aligned.

Cut the main miters

To cut the miters on the top panel, it helps a lot to have a track saw; I use a Festool 55. But you can get by with a good circular saw and a shopmade guide (drawing at left, facing page). You could also cut these miters on a tablesaw with a sliding table, if you have one. As to the miters on the edging pieces, I cut those on my tablesaw.

The project starts with a good selection of 4/4 stock. Choosing boards with lots of vertical grain makes it easier to produce a look at the ends of the table that mimics end grain. To create a seamless match of color and grain between the top panel and the side edging, I use wide boards for the first and last boards in the panel glue-up. To account for the edging and the return strips underneath, figure on gluing up a top panel about a foot longer and perhaps 8 in. wider than the finished top. Less overage is required on the sides, as the side returns can be cut from unmatched stock.

Once the top panel is glued up, cut the miters on the long sides. If you use a track-guided saw, make sure the cuts are parallel.

Next cut the miters on the ends of the panel. Use a square to align the track perpendicular to the sides, and mark each offcut to match the end it came from. The beauty of using these offcuts as edging—apart from the perfect grain match—is that they are already just the right length and have miters on the ends that will mate with the side edging. But they still need work.

Ensuring a square glue-up. It's key that the outside face of the edging and the top surface of the table form a 90° angle. Using biscuits helps with this, as does using both vertical and horizontal clamps. Edmundson screws on a temporary guide strip just behind the miter to seal the deal.

Glue One End at a Time

For maximum control of the miter joints, Edmundson glues on one piece at a time. He dry-clamps the opposite end for clamping purchase and to protect the sharp edge.

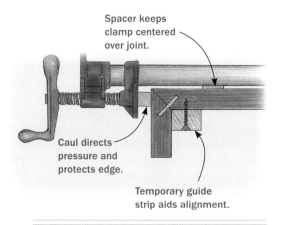

Spacer keeps clamp centered over joint.

Caul directs pressure and protects edge.

Temporary guide strip aids alignment.

TIP Use a guide strip. Screw down a straight strip right at the edge of the miter. This will help keep the edging at 90° as you clamp it on and also help to keep it from shifting inward.

First, at the tablesaw, with the blade vertical and the point of the miter riding against the fence, rip a clean edge parallel to the long miter (and save the offcut if you are planning to add return strips underneath the table). Then tilt the blade to 45° and run the clean edge against the fence to recut the miter. For a good grain match, you want to remove as little wood as possible from the top of the edging.

Test the fit of the miter joint to see that the edging forms a 90° angle with the top panel. If it doesn't, make a slight angle adjustment on the tablesaw and recut the miters. When the miter is right, rip the edging to width to create the faux table thickness you want.

Attach the end pieces first

I use biscuits in these joints, both for reinforcement and to help align the pieces during glue-up. The ends of the edging must line up correctly, so I place the first and last biscuits fairly close to the ends. For further help with alignment, I temporarily screw a strip of wood to the underside of the top, just behind the miter.

At glue-up I apply vertical pressure with quick-release clamps and horizontal pressure with bar clamps running the length of the tabletop. I use Gorilla glue for its longer open time. To play it safe, I glue one end at a time, dry-fitting the opposite end to protect the beveled edge. If I see gaps during the glue-up, I use the back of a chisel to burnish the corner slightly, crushing the grain so that the joint looks tight. It rounds the corner a bit, but no more than I will when I sand before finishing.

Side edging is next

Attaching the side edging is the next step, and it's a bit trickier. I use test pieces while fitting it. They let me dial in the angle of the miters on the ends of the edging, which may

not be exactly 45°. The test pieces don't need to be full length, just long enough to be safely cut on the tablesaw. Repeat the procedure from the end edging to produce edging and test pieces that are beveled on the top edge and ripped to width.

Now cut a 45° miter on both ends of your test piece, and slide one end into place on the table to see how it mates with the end edging. I make adjustments on the chopsaw until the fit is tight and then make notes on the angle. It might require a compound-angle cut. Repeat this process for the other three corners.

Now that you know the miter angles, you can cut one end of a piece of side edging, cut the other end a little long, and sneak up on the fit. Remember that at glue-up you'll be able to close small gaps by crushing the corner of the miter slightly.

When you've fitted both sides, cut biscuit joints and glue one side into place at a time, just as before. You don't need a guide strip this time, because the end edging will keep the side edging at 90°.

To add the return strips underneath the table, I start by gluing on a 2-in.-wide strip the full length of each side edging. Then I fill in the gap between these two strips with the offcut from the end edging. Last, I cut a piece of ¾-in.-thick plywood to fit roughly into the opening in the bottom of the faux slab—it doesn't have to fit perfectly. I screw the plywood to the base, and then, through slotted holes, I use pan-head screws with washers to attach the plywood to the underside of the tabletop.

Once your table is finished, I think you'll find that with a little cunning and some clean miter joints, you've made a massive-looking tabletop without breaking your back or your bank account.

Side pieces require test-fitting. The trick here is to use a test piece to gauge the actual miter angles at the ends of each side, which might not be perfect. Note the angles for each joint and then cut the real edging. To start, on a test piece that's mitered along the top edge, cut one end at a 45° angle, sawing at 90° to the length. If that fits perfectly, great. If not, make an adjustment to one or both of the angles at the chopsaw. Using the other end of the test piece, repeat the process to find the correct angle for the joint at the opposite end. Then cut the side edging to length.

Biscuit and glue the edging. Mark and biscuit the tabletop and edging. The glue-up process is the same as before: one piece at a time, with the opposite piece dry-fitted to protect the mitered edge.

Complete the illusion. When someone reaches under the tabletop, the return strips make it feel like a solid slab. Glue on the side strips first, then fill in between them at the ends. For the end returns, use offcuts from the ends of the panel so they expand and contract with the edging and the tabletop.

Glue on Return Strips

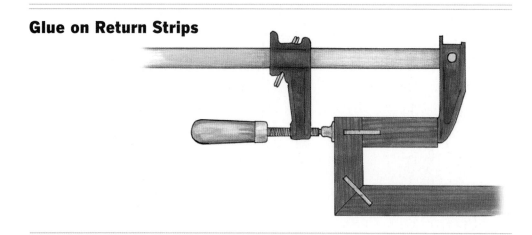

Learn to Resaw

TIMOTHY ROUSSEAU

Few techniques in woodworking can have as much impact on the design of your furniture as resawing. Resawing, the process of cutting thinner boards or veneers from thick stock, frees you from the dimensional constraints imposed on the board at the sawmill. Rather than compromising your design to work with the lumber as you bought it, you can saw the wood to create perfect boards for the project at hand.

The bandsaw is the ideal tool for this task, whether you have a 14-in. saw with 6 in. of resaw capacity or a 20-in. monster that can

handle boards 12 in. or wider. With the right setup, you can cut thin book-matched or slip-matched boards for a door panel, create frames with perfectly straight grain, or slice a gorgeous board into a stack of thin veneers, ready for a tabletop, drawer fronts, or case construction.

Ready your bandsaw for resawing

No matter what size saw you have, you won't resaw successfully if it isn't set up well. Especially important areas are the blade (sidebar, below), guides, and fence.

After putting the blade on the saw, many woodworkers fuss with centering it perfectly on the top wheel in an effort to eliminate drift, where the blade doesn't cut in a straight line. But that works only if the wheels are perfectly coplanar, which may not be the case with every saw. My simple approach is to get the blade aligned in center as best I can, set its tension, and then move on to the guides.

Get the guides right. After installing and tensioning the blade, adjust the thrust bearing and side guides so that they just kiss the blade. The side guides should be just behind the blade's gullets. This setup keeps the blade aligned and prevents binding.

You Don't Need a Fancy Blade

There are many blades designed for resawing— even some with carbide teeth—but it's hard to beat a ½-in.-wide, 3-tpi, carbon steel hook-tooth blade. This blade is great for hard- and softwoods, and does very well with rosewood, ebony, and other tough exotics. I prefer the hard-edge, flex-back blades from Sterling Saw (diamondsaw.com), which I buy from Mathieu Saws.

Spin the wheel. The blade should touch the guides intermittently. Bearing guides will spin off and on when set the right distance from the blade.

I can adjust the saw's fence to match the blade's drift later.

Every bandsaw has two sets of guides—one above and one below the table. Each set has two guides on the side of the blade and one behind it. Set up correctly, the guides keep the blade cutting straight without deflecting. Start with the top set. It's critical to get the guides as close as you can to the blade without them being in constant contact, which means that when the blade is spinning, the guides should touch it only intermittently. With bearing guides, you'll see the guide spin off and on. If you have block guides, listen for the sound of the blade running against them. Set up the side guides first, and then the thrust bearing. Set up the guides beneath the table last.

Add a resaw fence

A properly set up fence ensures that the veneers and boards you cut are of a consistent thickness. Most stock fences can be used to resaw narrow boards. My saw's fence is 2 in. tall, and I use it for boards up to 3 in. wide. For anything wider, I use an auxiliary fence clamped to the bandsaw table (see the drawing on p. 146). My fence is shaped like the letter L. The short leg is 6 in. tall and handles boards up to 8 in. wide, while the longer leg is 1 in. short of my saw's resaw capacity (13 in.), and I use it for boards wider than 8 in.

Snug the thrust bearing. Move it up until it begins to spin, then back it off a fuzz. When you spin the top wheel, the thrust bearing should spin intermittently.

Cut freehand along a straight line. Mark a line parallel to the board's edge and inset ¼ in. Cut at least 8 in. into the board. Taking care not to move the board, clamp it in place.

Align the fence to the board's edge. Slide the fence over until it touches the board along its length. Lock it down at that angle.

Use the saw's fence to position the auxiliary fence. Keep the auxiliary fence snug against the saw's fence as you set the width of cut (left), then clamp it in place (above).

Auxiliary Fence Handles Most Resawing

With two different-height fences, this fence can handle boards from 3 in. wide right up to your saw's capacity for resawing.

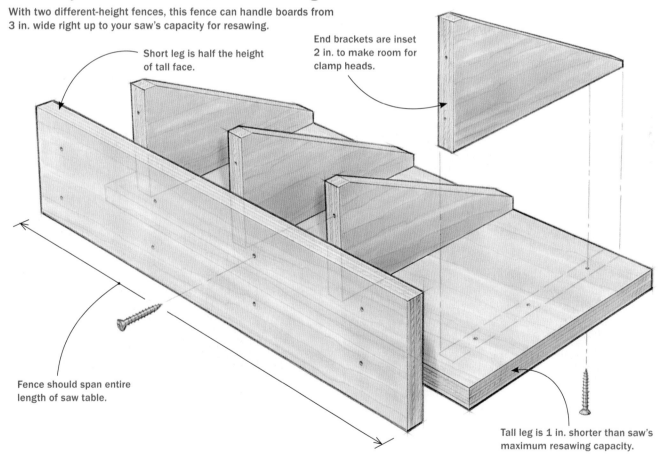

Short leg is half the height of tall face.

End brackets are inset 2 in. to make room for clamp heads.

Fence should span entire length of saw table.

Tall leg is 1 in. shorter than saw's maximum resawing capacity.

Clean and straight resaw cuts—ones that create veneer and boards with parallel faces—are impossible if the fence isn't parallel to the blade's drift, or the angle of its cut. Fortunately, adjusting the fence to account for drift is a simple process (see the bottom photos on p. 145).

Mill a board flat and square, and then draw a line down its length, ¼ in. from the edge. Cut along this line until the board is 8 in. or more past the blade. More than likely you'll notice that the board is slightly angled inward or outward. That angle shows which way the blade is drifting. Turn off the bandsaw, clamp the board in place, and bring the saw's fence up to the board's edge. Adjust the fence angle so that it touches the board along its full length. Lock it at that angle. The fence is now aligned to the blade's drift so that the saw will cut in a straight line.

Finally, make sure that the fence's vertical alignment is also parallel to the blade (sidebar, below). Otherwise, the veneer and boards you cut won't have parallel faces. If it's not, shim the base with blue tape.

Check for Vertical Alignment

Start by cutting a kerf into a scrap of wood (left). Then turn off the saw, bring the scrap to the top of the fence, and try to slide the kerf into the sawblade (center). If it doesn't align, shim the bottom of the fence with blue tape (right).

Get Better Cuts with Your Planer

JERRY C. FORSHEE

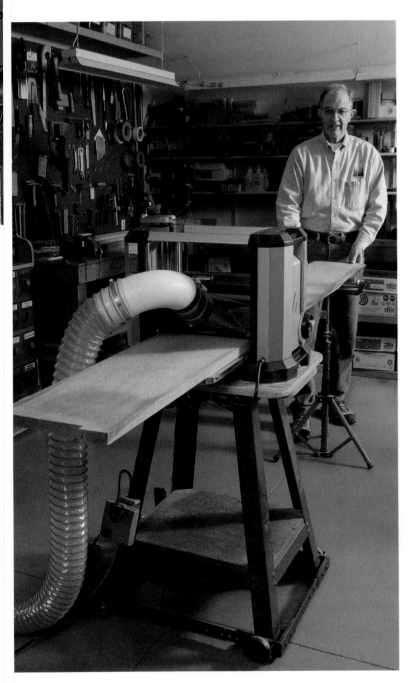

Precisely prepared stock, with a smooth surface and consistent thickness, is the foundation of quality woodworking. The planer is essential to that process.

It's important to understand that a planer does not flatten wood. Instead, the planer works in tandem with the jointer to flatten and square stock; neither can do the job of the other. The jointer is used first to surface one face flat, and the planer creates an opposite face smooth and parallel to it.

Set up your planer for success

Like other woodworking machines and tools, a planer must be well-tuned to do its job properly. Keep the knives clean and sharp, and change them when the planed stock's surface becomes irregular or grooved, when chipout becomes significant, and when the feed rate becomes noticeably more sluggish. The infeed and outfeed tables must be flat and in the same plane as the bed, and they must be smooth, clean, and treated with wax or dry, silicone-free lubricant for a low-friction surface. Dust collection is critical for personal health protection and ease of cleanup. It also can affect the quality of the cut, because unevacuated chips can dimple the face of the workpiece or get under the piece and cause an irregular cut.

Planer Anatomy

Thickness planers have a suspended cutterhead that creates a surface parallel to the bed. Infeed and outfeed rollers feed stock through the cutterhead and keep the material flat against the bed. Tables in front and back support the material as it enters and exits the machine.

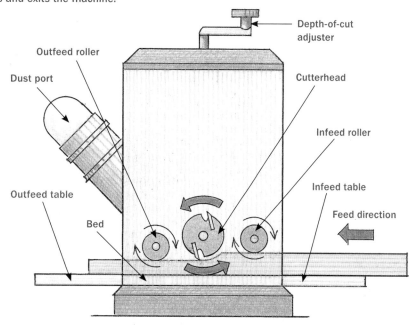

Depth-of-cut adjuster

Outfeed roller

Dust port

Cutterhead

Infeed roller

Outfeed table

Infeed table

Bed

Feed direction

Jointer before Planer

The planer doesn't flatten a board; it creates a surface that's parallel to the surface riding against the bed. One side of the board must be flattened at the jointer first. That flat face is the surface that rides against the bed.

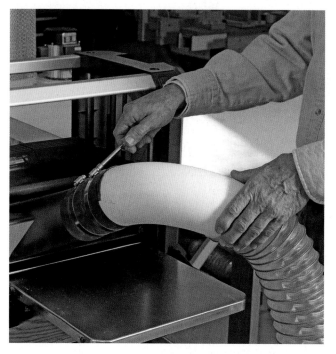

Use dust collection. The chips created by the planer are not only hazardous to your health, but they also can get trapped under incoming stock and cause an irregular cut with poor results.

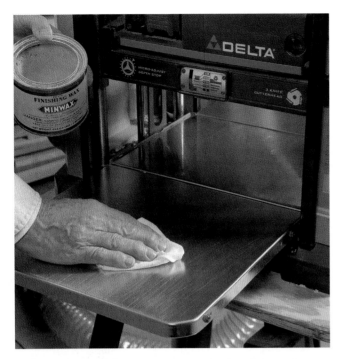

Make surfaces slick. Wood passing under the rollers applies a considerable amount of friction and pressure to the bed and tables. Applying wax to those surfaces will prevent things from bogging down.

Back to basics

While the planer seems to do the work for you, there are a few tips to help you get the best results.

Before you turn on the machine, identify the grain direction of the board. Look at the edge of the board and position it so that the grain runs downhill into the planer. Plane in the wrong direction and the machine will leave a rough, chipped-out surface.

Also, limit the depth of cut to 1/16 in. or less. This makes tearout less likely and reduces wear and tear on the motor. After setting the depth of cut, tighten down the cutterhead lock if present.

When planing, don't always feed boards into the center of the bed. Use the entire width of the cutterhead to even out knife wear and get a lot more life in between knife changes. Feed boards with difficult grain into

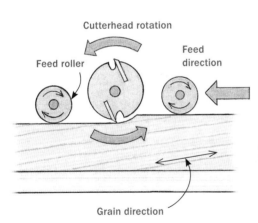

Pay attention to grain. The simplest way to avoid tearout is to carefully orient the grain before you feed any material into the planer. The grain should always be heading downhill into the machine.

the planer skewed at an angle, which helps create a cleaner shear cut across the grain.

Once both faces are parallel, remove material equally from both faces by flipping the workpiece, end for end, between passes to keep proper grain orientation. This removes material equally from both sides, which helps the board remain flat.

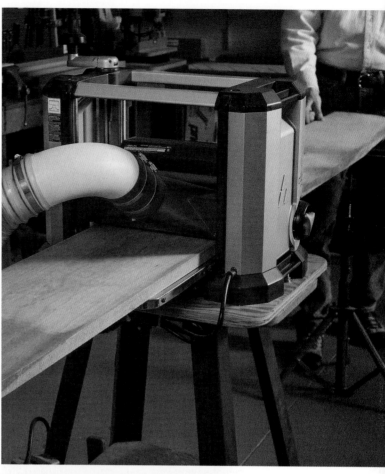

Take a light cut. Set the depth of cut for less than ¹⁄₁₆ in. to reduce the likelihood of tearout (above). This is especially important on wide stock, which can bog down the smaller motors on benchtop planers (right).

Skew the board. For boards with tricky grain, feed the board at a slight angle. This creates a shearing cut across the grain that reduces tearout.

Gang up the parts. Running separate boards through the planer directly behind one another eliminates snipe from the boards in the center.

What Is Snipe?

Snipe occurs at the beginning or end of a cut, when one end of the board is unsupported by a feed roller. The feed roller that's engaged with the board will lift it into the cutterhead and cause the knives to take a bigger bite.

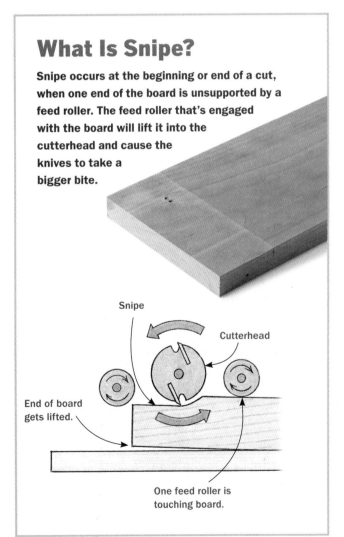

Snipe

Cutterhead

End of board gets lifted.

One feed roller is touching board.

Tips for avoiding snipe

We've all seen snipe—that ugly gouge on the leading or trailing end of the board. It happens when the stock is not supported by both the infeed roller and the outfeed roller at the same time (drawing, left).

One of the simplest ways to avoid snipe is to lift up on the trailing end of the board as it enters the machine and then on the leading end on the outfeed side as it exits. This keeps the end of the board that is not supported by the opposite feed roller flat to the bed. You also can start with a workpiece that is extra long and then cut off the snipe at each end. Or, snipe can be reduced by feeding boards through the planer butted end to end. This keeps the feed roller tension equalized. This "planer train" technique can also be used to control shorter stock.

Edge-planing stock

Stock that has already been milled to have parallel sides and relatively smooth edges can be planed on edge to fine-tune the width and yield smooth edges.

If you are going to try this, the maximum width of the stock should be equal to, or less

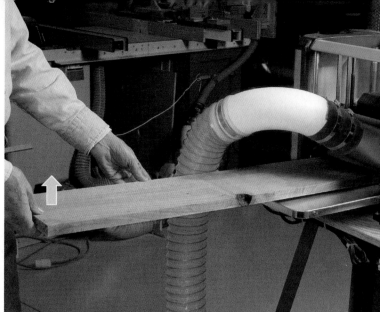

Lift the ends on the way in. As the board enters the planer, its leading end is not supported by the outfeed roller. Lifting the trailing end keeps the leading end planted against the bed.

And on the way out. The same applies for the board as it exits the planer. Lift the leading end to keep the trailing end from rising into the cutterhead.

than, five times the thickness of the stock. For 1-in.-thick stock, the board should be 5 in. wide or less. This keeps the stock from being pressed over and out of square by the feed rollers. When I plane stock this way, I feed it through in small bundles (photos, below). This helps keep the boards upright and feeding at the same rate. Also, always use the centermost portion of the planer. On some planers, the feed rollers are spring-loaded on the ends and can cause the stock to tip.

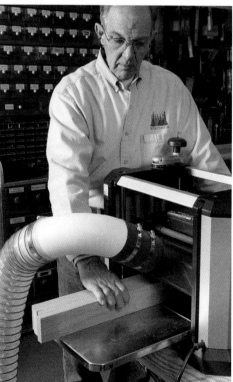

Group narrow parts. Edge-planing narrow stock isn't just difficult, it can be dangerous. Avoid accidents by planing on edge. When you need consistent and dead-accurate widths for multiple components, edge-planing gives great results. As he feeds the parts into the planer, Forshee holds them firmly to keep them upright and together in the center of the bed (far left). He then transfers his grip to the outfeed side (left).

Lengthen short stock. For stock that's too short to plane, glue hardwood runners to the edges. This effectively increases the length of the board so that it can be grabbed by both feed rollers, as well as keeping snipe from the short length of material.

Flatten Stock that's Too Wide for Your Jointer

The planer isn't a jointer, but when you need to flatten stock that's too wide or wild for your jointer, the planer can get the job done safely and fast. While the planer and jointer are best used as a team, sometimes a board is too wide, too heavy, or just too cupped and bowed to be flattened efficiently on the jointer. The solution is a simple planer sled that's reusable and easy to set up in minutes.

The sled is a sheet of ¾-in. plywood or MDF, just narrower than the capacity of the planer and as long as you need it to be. A short hardwood cleat glued at the trailing edge keeps the sled and the stock on it moving at the same pace.

Setting up the sled is easy. Put the stock on the sled with the end against the cleat. Use wood shims to stabilize the board from rocking and then under any spots where the board is off the sled. It's best to keep stock removal even across the board, so don't over-shim on one end or side but rather spread out the difference over the board. Once the shims are in place, attach them with hot glue. Then trim the shims so that they don't overhang the sled sides.

Just like normal stock, run the stock and sled through the planer and take light passes until the top face is flat. Then remove the stock from the sled, flip it over, and plane the opposite face.

Trim the shim. Cut the shims with a handsaw, making sure they're well inside the edge of the sled to avoid any hangups as the sled passes through the planer.

Shim the stock flat. While on the sled, use shims to stop the board from rocking.

Keep the shims in place. To keep the shims from shifting while the sled is inside the planer, use hot glue. A single, thick bead where the shim and board meet is usually enough to hold it down.

Flatten it slowly. Feed the sled and board through the planer, taking light cuts. When one face is flat, remove the board from the sled and plane the opposite face flat and parallel.

Drill Press Tips and Tricks

MICHAEL FORTUNE

Set up properly, any drill press can create clean, accurate holes, small and large, in workpieces of all shapes and sizes. Armed with a few accessories, though, it can do much more. Over my 40 years of woodworking, I've developed a series of tips and jigs that will make the drill press one of your favorite shop companions. They will

Do More with Your Drill Press

USE A NO-FRILLS FENCE AND TABLE
Fortune prefers a simple MDF table and hardwood fence, clamping both down in one shot. To change the fence setting slightly, loosen the table bracket and pivot the whole table on the column.

Two-faced. Fortune's shopmade fence is machined straight and square. It can be used tall or short, letting you raise the table for small bits without interfering with the crank handles. He puts a ⅛-in. rabbet along the bottom edges so dust doesn't push the workpiece away, and glues 120-grit sandpaper to the bottom faces to keep the fence from shifting.

GET A SET OF SUPPORT ARMS
Rather than using a large table to support long workpieces, Fortune sticks with the small table, plus a set of work-support arms. The rollers extend outward up to 28 in. on each side and are easily raised and lowered to keep the workpiece level on the table, or slid inboard to save space. The mounting bracket holds more securely if you place small wood blocks at the end of the straps.

work with any drill press, big or small, fancy or basic.

Success starts with your setup. A lot of woodworkers buy or make a big auxiliary table to support large workpieces. But these offer false security. They are rarely flat, and they obstruct your ability to get in close and see where you want to drill a hole. They include a replaceable insert in the middle, sitting in a rabbet that needs frequent cleaning. These big tables also make it hard to get clamps close to the bit, so they need T-tracks and awkward hold-downs.

The solution is elegantly simple. I use sacrificial 12-in. squares of MDF as backer boards. Like table inserts, they prevent blowout on the back of the hole. The difference is that they can simply be shifted to expose a fresh surface and discarded when they look like Swiss cheese.

Workpieces always lie flat on this small work surface, and clamping is a lot easier. It

SHINE A LIGHT

Overhead light gets blocked by the head of the machine. The solution is a magnetic, adjustable work light, which floods the workspace and makes it easier to hit the mark.

RAISE THE WORK ZONE

Bring the work closer to your eyes to increase the tool's accuracy. If you have a benchtop model, put it on a higher table (photo, left); raise a floor model by putting it on a mobile base or low platform. Fortune locates the table so that the workpiece is about a foot from his eyes.

ADD A STOP

Like his fence, Fortune's stop blocks have sandpaper below and a small rabbet on the working face to give dust a place to go.

means making your own fences and stops, but those work better too, as you'll see. The small table won't support long workpieces, but I'll show you how to deal with that.

After you nail the basic setup, there are quite a few great accessories for the drill press, some bought and some made. I'll tell you which ones really matter.

Tricks for holding work of any size

Small parts. It is unsafe to hold small parts in your hand. To secure them for safe drilling, pivot the table to clamp these small pieces near the edge (photo, below left). Use a wooden hand screw with various notches cut into it to hold short pieces upright (photo, below right).

Clamp near the edge. Pivot the table to clamp small workpieces like these tabletop buttons.

Doctor a hand screw. To hold short pieces upright, Fortune uses a notched wooden hand screw.

Long parts. To drill into the end of a long part, you rotate the table sideways, but there is a surprising amount of force required to cut into end grain and you need a way to secure the workpiece solidly. The jig (drawing, right) includes both a sliding T-fence to locate the part and an adjustable stop to keep it from shifting downward.

End-Grain Drilling Jig

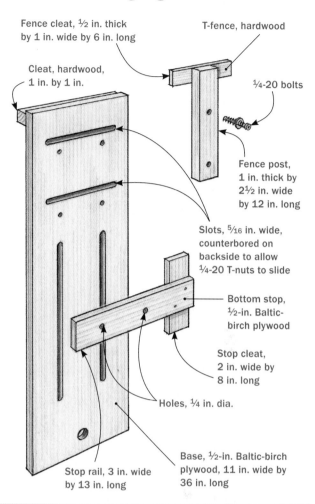

Fence cleat, ½ in. thick by 1 in. wide by 6 in. long

T-fence, hardwood

Cleat, hardwood, 1 in. by 1 in.

¼-20 bolts

Fence post, 1 in. thick by 2½ in. wide by 12 in. long

Slots, ⁵⁄₁₆ in. wide, counterbored on backside to allow ¼-20 T-nuts to slide

Bottom stop, ½-in. Baltic-birch plywood

Stop cleat, 2 in. wide by 8 in. long

Holes, ¼ in. dia.

Base, ½-in. Baltic-birch plywood, 11 in. wide by 36 in. long

Stop rail, 3 in. wide by 13 in. long

Align it first. Fortune places a long rod in the chuck to get the jig plumb (right). You can use the jig to drill accurate dowel holes in the ends of parts, or use a giant plug cutter to form a tenon as shown (above).

Jig for big holes

A circle-cutter makes clean and accurate disks and holes up to 6 in. dia., to accept a shop-vacuum hose, for example. The circle-cutter I use is made by General Tools. It has a standard twist drill bit in the center, which keeps the outer cutter on track.

Measuring trick. To cut a hole, turn the cutting tool so the tip faces outward, and measure from the edge of the bit to the tip. The bit is ¼ in. dia., so add ⅛ in. to get the true radius.

Safety first. Use these cutters at or below 500 rpm, always clamp down the workpiece, and be very careful to keep hands and clamps away from the spinning arm.

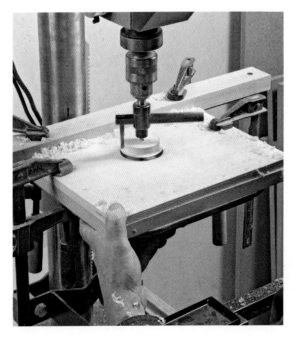

Easy does it. Lower the cutter steadily until the disk in the middle is freed and starts to spin. Then just lift it out. On thick workpieces, go halfway through and then drill a ¼-in. hole all the way through so you can finish the job from the other side.

Sanding specialist

Flap sanders are an underappreciated accessory and are great for sanding odd-shaped items and highlighting grain. There are disposable models, but I prefer the type that has a roll of sandpaper in the middle, which can be unwound and torn off to refresh the flaps.

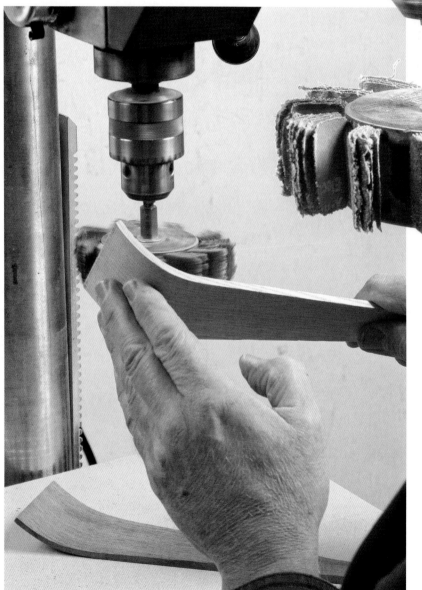

Solid sandpaper softens. Choose a solid roll of paper, and use it to smooth 3-D curves and soften the edges of small parts, like these salad tongs, which were bent on a hot pipe.

Rust remover

Buy an inexpensive set of wire brushes to clean rust off metal parts and tools (top photo, facing page). Sets come with a variety of sizes to fit into any nook or cranny. Run wire brushes at medium to slow speed.

Threaded holes, too

Woodworkers occasionally have to drill and thread a hole in wood or metal. It's called tapping a hole. After drilling, the trick is to get the tap to start true and straight. You can start it by hand, using a tap handle, but the drill press guarantees success (bottom photos, facing page).

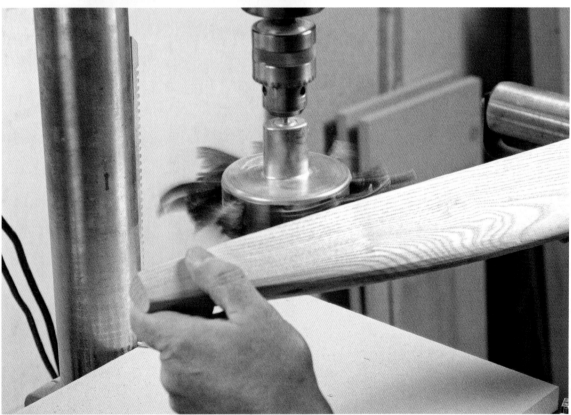

Perforated paper adds texture. This type of sandpaper acts as a row of thin strips (top). Use it to emphasize the grain of ring-porous woods. The texture is subtle in harder woods like oak or ash (above) and more pronounced in softer woods like cypress and cedar, for example.

Get rid of rust. Wire brushes can be used to clean rust off metal parts and tools. An inexpensive set is all you need to get the job done.

Good start. Put the tap in the chuck and rotate it by hand while applying gentle downward pressure with the crank handle. Go in a couple of threads, and then turn it backward to withdraw the tap.

Finish by hand. Attach a tap wrench and finish the job. After every couple of turns, reverse the tap to break the chip.

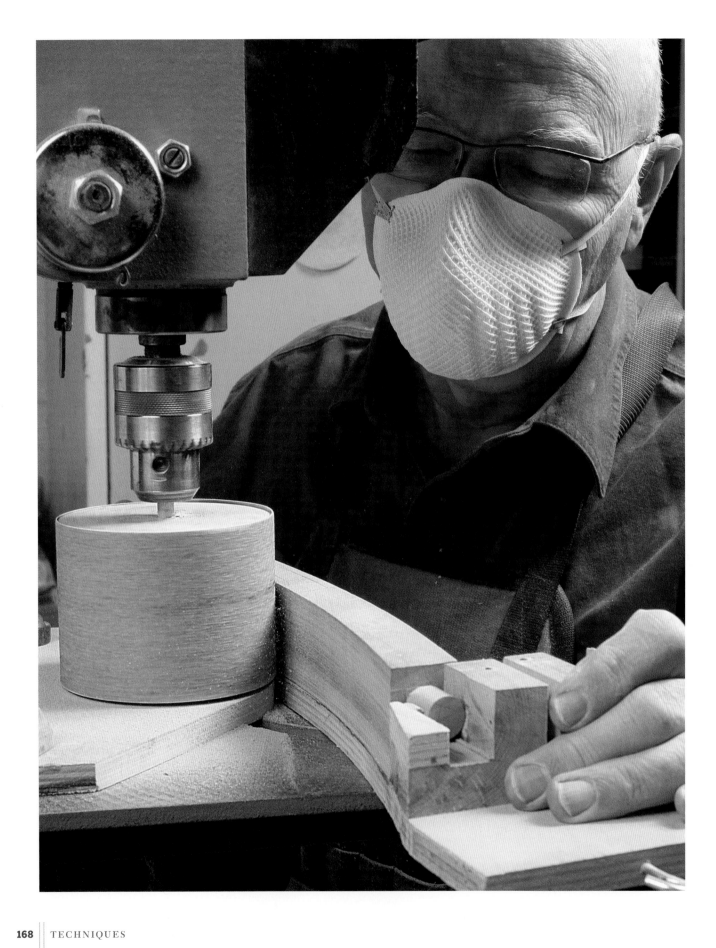

Sanding on the Drill Press

MICHAEL FORTUNE

When I bought my first drill press, I discovered that those sanding drums that go in the chuck and accept abrasive sleeves let me sand all sorts of inside curves, whether on templates or actual workpieces. But the sleeves were available in a limited range of grits, the abrasive wore out quickly, and they weren't cheap. And the drums were too small in diameter for a lot of my needs.

So I make my own drums out of plywood disks and wrap high-quality cloth-backed sandpaper around them, attaching it with spray adhesive. I can make them any size and they work beautifully.

The larger the drum, the more surface area, and the longer the sandpaper lasts. Larger drums also leave a less bumpy surface. I've made drums up to 8 in. dia., though most are closer to 4 in., fitting a wider variety of curves while still leaving a relatively smooth surface.

By the way, while the bearings in a drill press are not designed for heavy sideways pressure, as they would be in a true milling machine, they handle light to medium lateral pressure just fine.

For the sandpaper, I buy 80-grit sanding belts, made for belt sanders, from my hardware store and cut them as required. I sometimes use a lower grit to remove stock more quickly or a higher one for a smoother finish.

Sanding curves is just the beginning for these shopmade drums. I'll show you how I turn the drum into a thickness sander for thin strips and a pattern sander for flawless curved parts. But let's start with the drum itself.

Make your own drums

To make the drums, I cut a series of disks from ¾-in.-thick plywood. I've had good luck with a circle-cutter made by General Tools. Be sure to turn the tip the right way for cutting disks (vs. cutting holes) and use a very slow speed, under 500 rpm, if possible.

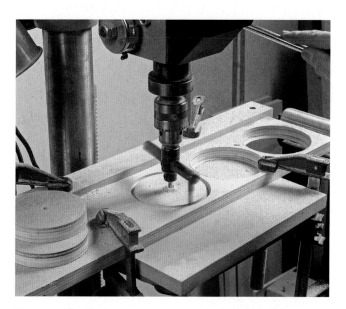

Bang out the drum. Cut and stack a few plywood circles to make any size sanding drum. Large drums work well for smoother curves, while smaller drums get into tighter spaces. To make disks (vs. holes), use a circle cutter, turning the tip of the cutter inward. Set the radius, measure from the bit to the cutter, and add ⅛ in., half the diameter of the bit. Clamp down the plywood each time, and sand the tearout off the edges of each circle.

Glue the stack. Use a ¼-in.-dia. rod or drill bit to align the circles as you glue them together. Wax the rod or bit to resist glue, and try chucking it in a drill to help you insert it. With the rod or bit in place, clamp the circles into a stack.

The circle-cutter leaves a ¼-in.-dia. hole through the center of each disk. To align the disks as you glue them into a stack, insert a ¼-in.-dia. rod or drill bit through the hole. Wax the rod to make it easier to remove once the glue is set.

The sandpaper goes into a small bandsawn slot. You need to slightly round the leading edge of the slot, so the sandpaper rolls smoothly into the leading edge without a bump.

Add the shank and smooth the outside of the drum (left photos, facing page). Last, varnish the outside of the drum, making it easier to clean off the spray adhesive that will attach the sandpaper.

Slot it. Cut a shallow slot on the bandsaw (left), to accommodate the end of the sandpaper. The outside of the slot gets a small roundover on one corner (above).

Leading Edge Needs a Curve

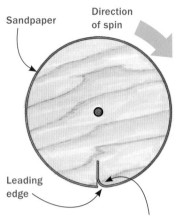

Sandpaper

Direction of spin

Leading edge

Curve lets the sandpaper turn the corner without creating a bump.

Sandpaper goes on easily

Cut a strip of cloth-backed sandpaper the same width as the drum. Always turn sandpaper upside down to cut it with a knife. Slip one end of the paper in the slot, wrap it around the drum, mark it, and cut it to length.

Use spray adhesive, or contact cement, following the manufacturer's directions, to affix the paper snugly to the drum. When the paper wears out, just peel it off and remove the old adhesive with lacquer thinner.

Add a shank. Fortune mounts a ⁵⁄₁₆-in.-dia. lag screw in the drill press, rotating the chuck by hand so the lag screw enters the wood straight. Then he cuts off the head with a hacksaw.

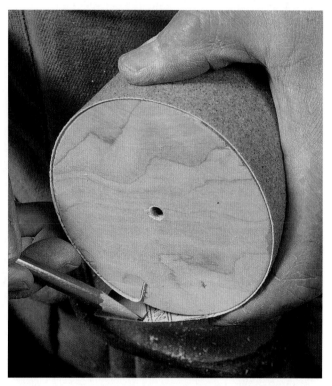

Attach the sandpaper. Fortune uses 60- and 80-grit cloth-backed sandpaper, harvested from sanding belts and attached with spray-on adhesive. To start, mark and cut the paper. Dry-fit the paper and mark its length. Then tear or cut it to size.

Sand and seal. Chuck the drum in the drill press and smooth it using a sanding block and 80-grit paper. Add varnish to make the adhesive easy to remove later. Don't use lacquer; the adhesive will dissolve it.

Spray and wrap. Spray a thin coat of adhesive onto the drum and paper (left), let it get tacky for a few minutes, and then wrap on the paper, starting in the groove (top) and continuing to the end (above).

TIP When you are not using the drum, a few rubber bands will keep the sandpaper attached until next time.

Add a simple sanding table

Some drill-press tables have room for a drum to drop below the surface, but usually not far. My auxiliary table allows the sanding drum to be positioned at a variety of heights so the entire surface can be used, extending the life of the abrasive.

Cut a hole in the center of a plywood panel, just larger than the largest drum you'll use. Next, screw on two runners that have cutouts for clamp heads. Adding two more plywood pieces, one with a large hole for a shop-vacuum hose, creates an efficient dust-collection system.

Make a New Table

An auxiliary table with a hole for the drum allows you to raise and lower the drum to use the entire width of abrasive.

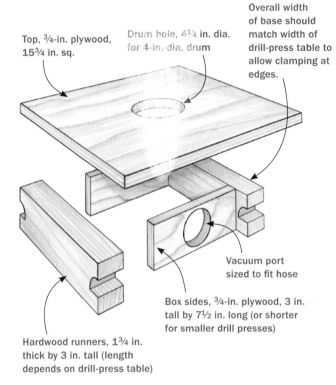

Top, ¾-in. plywood, 15¾ in. sq.

Drum hole, 4¼ in. dia. for 4-in.-dia. drum

Overall width of base should match width of drill-press table to allow clamping at edges.

Vacuum port sized to fit hose

Box sides, ¾-in. plywood, 3 in. tall by 7½ in. long (or shorter for smaller drill presses)

Hardwood runners, 1¾ in. thick by 3 in. tall (length depends on drill-press table)

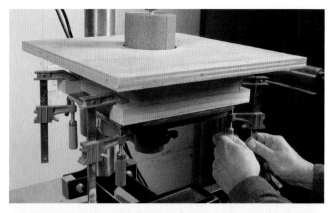

Quick setup. Raise the drill-press table so the drum drops into the hole. Then clamp the sanding table in place (top) and attach a shop vacuum (above). Cut very close to the line on the bandsaw, then feed the workpiece into the drum's rotation (below) for heavy removal. You can sand the piece very lightly with the rotation to smooth small bumps.

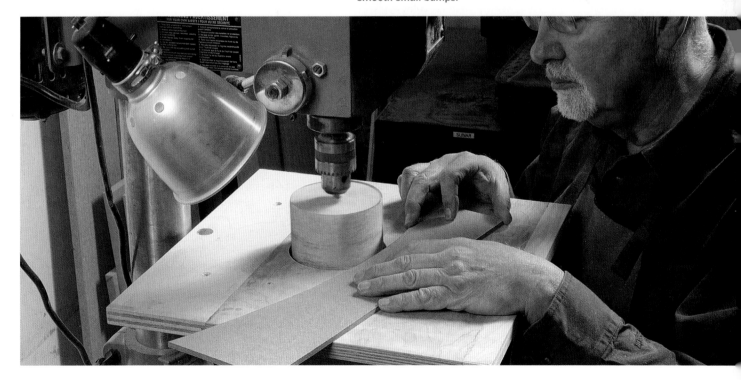

Plane thin strips. Clamping a simple fence to your sanding table lets you drum-sand material that is too thin for the thickness planer. Glue sandpaper to the bottom of the fence to keep it from shifting under pressure. Bandsaw the material close to size, and position the fence to press a piece against the drum as shown. Then remove the material, loosen one clamp, and bump that end of the fence toward the drum.

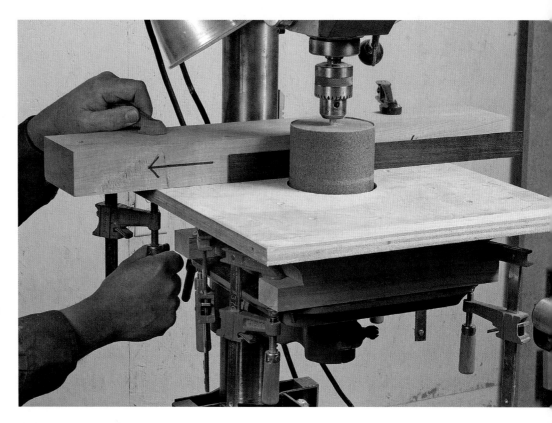

Add a fence for thin strips

Not long after I began using the sanding drum, I realized I could put a fence behind it to create smooth inlay material. Thin strips are fed into the space between the drum and the fence, always against the rotation of the drum.

The parts should be bandsawn very close to the finished thickness, say just ¹⁄₆₄ in. thicker, or the sandpaper will clog or burn. Use the lowest speed and 100-grit paper. After the inlay is glued in, take a first pass with a paint scraper to remove a layer of wood and any sanding grit along with it.

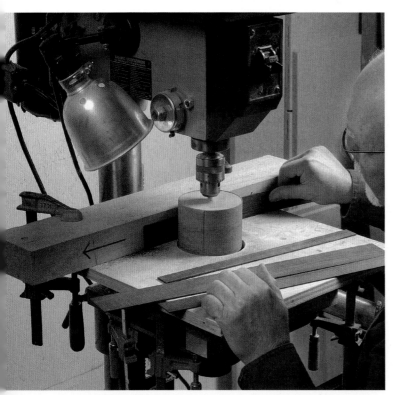

Against the spin. Feed the stock against the drum's rotation. Otherwise, it will become a tiny missile.

Set the tip. If you have bandsawn the workpiece close to the line, set the tip of the pattern guide flush with the drum. If you have big bumps or lots of waste to remove, set the tip a bit proud for the first pass or two.

Sand to a Pattern

Add a template guide under the drum, and it becomes a pattern sander, helping you duplicate curved parts the way a shaper would.

PATTERN GUIDE

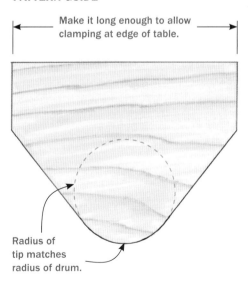

Make it long enough to allow clamping at edge of table.

Radius of tip matches radius of drum.

Turn the drum into a pattern sander

Before I owned a shaper, this is how I did all of my curved parts. Just cut the curve close on the bandsaw and then finish the job on this simple jig, which registers against a pattern. If you set it up carefully, the jig will also finish-sand a routed surface.

The pattern is attached to the workpiece in any number of ways, from toggle clamps to double-sided tape. The pattern guide is clamped to the table. Its nose has the same diameter as the drum, and it can be moved in or out to adjust the amount of wood removed.

For the smoothest surface, always choose the largest possible sanding drum (and pattern guide) that will follow the shape of your workpiece. The plywood drum will create a square, accurate edge.

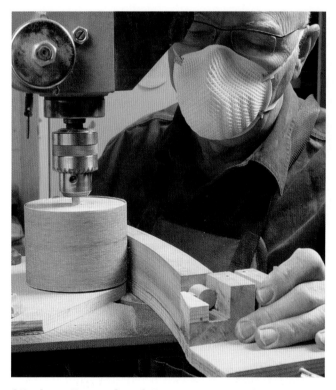

Attach a pattern and sand. There are a number of ways to attach a pattern to your workpiece, from double-sided tape to toggle clamps to this jig that captures the round tenons on the ends of chair parts. Feed the workpiece against the direction of the drum.

Get Started with Your Plunge Router

JEFF MILLER

The router is one of the most versatile tools in the shop. Of the two main types, the plunge model trumps the fixed-base variety, at least for me. It handles everything its more basic cousin can, adding the very useful ability to plunge in and out of the work on the fly. This means that in addition to grooves, dadoes, and edge moldings, you'll also be able to rout mortises, cut stopped grooves and dadoes, excavate grooves and recesses for inlay, and create a variety of decorative piercings.

As for choosing a plunge router, I recommend buying one with at least 12 amps of power. A smaller motor can bog down during heavier tasks like mortising. It's best to hold a router in your hands before buying it. You should be able to keep your hands on the handles at all times when working. That's why plunge routers have both the on/off switch and the plunge lock either on the handles or a finger's reach away. Each manufacturer takes a slightly different approach, so make sure you can easily stop the tool and lock and unlock the plunge mechanism while maintaining control.

Constant control. You need to be able to reach the key controls without taking your hands off the handles. On this plunge router, the on/off switch is in one handle, while the plunge lock is easily accessible with the thumb of the other hand.

Upgrade your straight bit. Normal straight bits (far right) are fine for many router cuts, but a solid-carbide, up-spiral bit (right) works much better for plunge cuts because it clears chips as you rout.

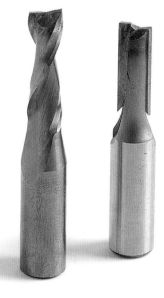

How to make clean mortises

One of the tasks a plunge router does best is make smooth, accurate mortises for strong joinery. Making this challenging cut is a good place to introduce my approach to plunge-routing.

There are many ways to control a router for safe and accurate movement. For mortising, I generally use an edge guide, an accessory that attaches to the base and rides the edge of the workpiece, letting you rout in a straight line parallel to that edge.

If the fence on your edge guide is shorter than 12 in., add a longer wooden fence to it. The extra length will make it easier to maintain contact with the workpiece throughout the cut.

Other than those situations where you're using the router as a fixed-base tool, such as when you are molding an edge with a bearing-guided bit, you'll always want to start and finish a cut with the router bit raised out of the cut and locked. Think of this as "the upright and locked position for takeoff and landing."

Simple way to set the depth of cut. Mark the depth line on the outside of the workpiece, plunge the bit to the line, and then lock the plunge lever. Now lower the depth-stop rod against one of the stops on the turret below, and lock it. Finally, raise the bit and follow the steps here.

Align the bit. Miller lays out the mortises in pencil, and then adjusts the edge guide so the bit lines up with his layout lines.

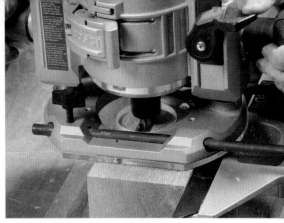

Go lightly. With the bit just above the workpiece, turn on the router. Lower the bit roughly 1⁄16 in., lock the plunge lever, and make a light cut, stopping at the end line.

The job goes quickly. At the end of each pass, unlock the plunge lever and lower the bit by feel, roughly 1⁄16 in. each time. Make passes until the depth stop bottoms out.

Push against the Guide

Put the edge guide on the same side of the workpiece as your body, and push against it to keep the router bit from wandering.

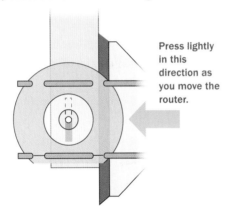

Press lightly in this direction as you move the router.

Take Light Passes

Don't overtax the router, and you'll get much less vibration and cleaner results.

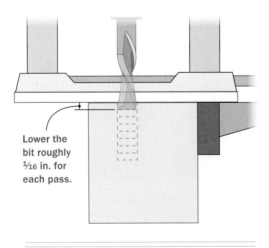

Lower the bit roughly 1⁄16 in. for each pass.

Now to the plunge action. Routers cut much more cleanly with a series of light passes, rather than one deep one. That's why plunge routers have a system of multiple depth stops. The idea is to preset each stop, and switch from one to the other between passes. But I don't think the multiple stops are worth the trouble. For one thing, I find that the steps between stops make the router take too heavy a cut for my liking. Also, on most routers, you can't switch stops without removing your hands from one of the handles, which is unsafe unless you first turn off the router. So I simply set the final depth of cut with any one of the stops, and then work down to it with a series of very shallow passes controlled by feel. The work goes faster, and the final results are better.

As for where to start and stop each pass, you can trust your pencil marks or you can place stop blocks atop the workpiece.

T-square jig makes dadoes

To make a dado, which is a groove across a board or panel, an edge guide usually won't work. That's because most dadoes are too far from a parallel edge. The simplest approach is to use a shopmade T-square. Clamped to a board with its fence snug to the edge, the T-square jig provides a straight edge that guides the router base.

Use a T-square jig for dadoes. A simple right-angle cutting guide will make dadoes of all kinds, whether all the way across a workpiece or stopped short of the edge. Setup is a cinch. After using the jig just once, you create a slot in the fence that can be used to align the jig with layout marks.

Choose a router bit that's the size of the dado you want. Start by clamping the T-square jig to a scrap piece and routing a slot in the fence. This will tell you where all future cuts will line up, as long as you use that same bit.

Now lay out the workpiece and set the location of the T-square accordingly. Set the depth of cut and rout.

Two tips. Use a series of light passes again. If you gang up the sides of a bookcase, you can rout two corresponding dadoes at once.

Push against the Fence

Again, press lightly against the fence to keep the router from wandering.

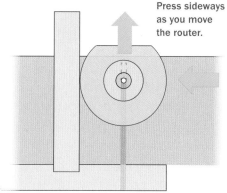

Press sideways as you move the router.

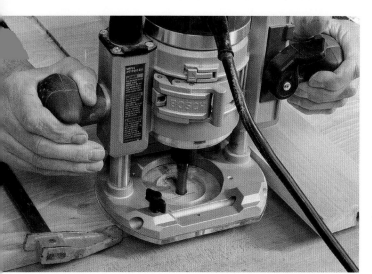

Stopped cuts are simple. For dadoes that need to stop before reaching an edge, just stop at a layout line and raise the bit out of the cut.

Go freehand for inlay. A router usually needs some type of guidance system, but you can work freehand when roughing out a pocket for a small inlay like this butterfly key. Stick the inlay on the surface. Put a couple of small dots of yellow glue on the bottom and press it down firmly where you want it. Wait 20 minutes for the glue to set. Double-sided tape is also a good option.

Now knife around it. Start with a very light pass to establish the line and then deepen it. Afterward, darken the lines with a fine pencil to make them more visible.

Router removes the waste. Pop off the inlay piece and begin routing in the center of the recess in overlapping passes, stopping 1/16 in. or so from the layout lines.

Rout freehand for a decorative inlay

Routing a shallow pocket for an inlay is one place where you can use the router without a guide system. The easiest method for laying out the cut is simply to stick the inlay to the workpiece temporarily and scribe around it with a marking knife. Then you just pry off the inlay, set the depth of cut a little shallower than the inlay itself, and stay slightly inside the lines as you rout. Follow with a chisel (photo, right).

There are other great ways to use your plunge router, such as adding a set of guide bushings that can be used with an endless variety of shopmade templates, but I'll leave those for another time.

Chisel work finishes the job. Don't start chopping right in the scribe lines or the cavity will end up too big. Nibble away the waste, ending with a light chop in the scribe line.

Inlay drops right in. When the fit is good, apply glue and tap the inlay into place. Wait a day for the glue to fully dry, and then use a handplane to level the inlay with the surface.

Easy Angled Tenons with a Router Jig

JEFF MILLER

Chair joinery is a challenge. Many of the joints are angled, and all of them are subjected to powerful stresses when the chair is in use. To contend with these issues, I almost always choose the mortise-and-tenon joint. If the joints are angled, I prefer to cut straight mortises and then angle the tenons.

The tricky part is cutting the angled tenons. But the jig presented here, used with a plunge router fitted with a straight bit and guide bushing, greatly simplifies the task. With an upright that clamps in your vise, a platform that supports the router, and a template that guides the bushing, the jig enables you to cut the two main cheeks and

How the Jig Works

CHAIR GEOMETRY

A typical chair narrows at the back, creating an angle at each side seat-rail joint.

Splay angle

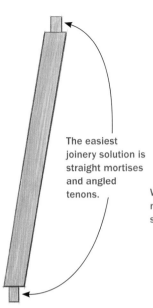

The easiest joinery solution is straight mortises and angled tenons.

WEDGE HANDLES THE ANGLED TENONS

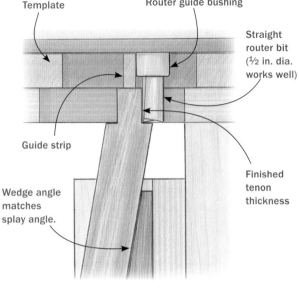

Template

Router guide bushing

Straight router bit (½ in. dia. works well)

Guide strip

Finished tenon thickness

Wedge angle matches splay angle.

shoulders of an angled tenon in a single, stable setup. Then, using the routed shoulders as a reference, you can finish the tenon with a bit of simple chisel work. The jig works equally well for straight tenons.

The template is removable, and you'll want to make separate templates for tenons of different thicknesses. The wedge that holds the workpiece at the correct angle is also removable, so you can use different wedges depending on the tenon angle you want.

Take care with the template

The base of the jig is straightforward and quick to build, but slow down when you get to the template. I glue it up from three parts—two notched side pieces and a guide strip between them. The router's bushing will ride on both sides of the guide strip to produce the tenon, so the strip must be sized accurately. To determine its thickness, start with the thickness of the tenon you want and subtract the difference between the guide

Simple Router Jig for Tenons

Easy to make and simple to use, this router jig will crank out perfect-fitting tenons (angled or straight) with perfectly aligned shoulders. The top plate supports the router and orients the template (drawing, p. 184). If the top plate is aligned with the L-fence below, the tenons will be square and accurate.

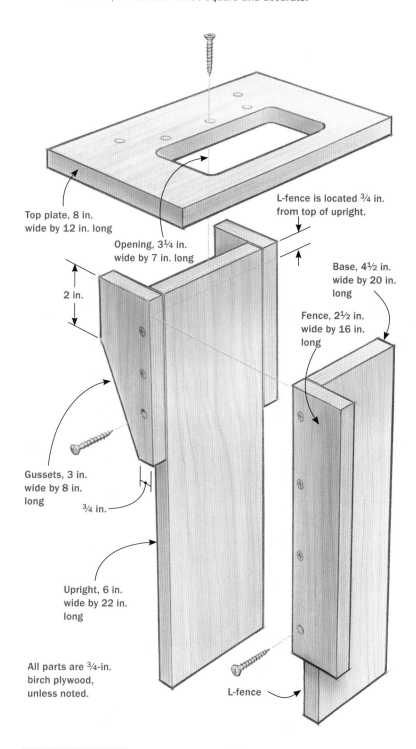

Top plate, 8 in. wide by 12 in. long

Opening, 3¼ in. wide by 7 in. long

L-fence is located ¾ in. from top of upright.

2 in.

Base, 4½ in. wide by 20 in. long

Fence, 2½ in. wide by 16 in. long

Gussets, 3 in. wide by 8 in. long

¾ in.

Upright, 6 in. wide by 22 in. long

All parts are ¾-in. birch plywood, unless noted.

L-fence

Gussets go on flush. If the gussets are square and you attach them flush to the upright, the top plate will go on square. Clamp the gussets as you screw them on.

Square the top plate side to side. Drive a single screw in the middle, square the edges of the top plate with the upright below, and then clamp and add the remaining screws.

Now the L-fence. Screw the L-fence together and then attach it to the upright, squaring it to the top plate before clamping and screwing it down. Be sure the L-fence sits well below the top for router-bit clearance.

bushing and router bit. For example, if you're using a ⅝-in.-dia. bushing with a ½-in.-dia. bit (a difference of ⅛ in.) and want a ½-in.-thick tenon, make the guide strip ⅜ in. thick.

Start by notching the two side pieces, and then mill the strip. To dial in the thickness of the guide strip, dry-clamp the template and use it to cut a test tenon. If the tenon doesn't fit the mortise perfectly, either plane the strip a bit thinner or make a new, slightly thicker one. When the tenon fits the mortise perfectly, glue the strip into the template.

Once the template is glued up, add the rails, which register the template square to

Accurate Template is the Heart of the Jig

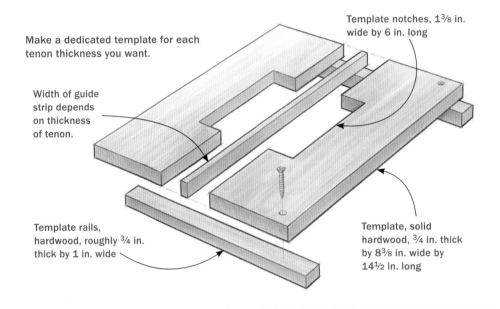

Make a dedicated template for each tenon thickness you want.

Width of guide strip depends on thickness of tenon.

Template notches, 1⅜ in. wide by 6 in. long

Template rails, hardwood, roughly ¾ in. thick by 1 in. wide

Template, solid hardwood, ¾ in. thick by 8⅜ in. wide by 14½ in. long

Dial in the strip. To size the guide strip, take the difference in size between the bit and bushing, and subtract that from the desired tenon thickness. Plane the guide strip to that dimension or just a bit over.

Give the template a dry run. Clamp the template parts together dry, attach the template to the jig, insert a workpiece, and cut a tenon (1). Test the tenon in its mortise (2). If you are happy with the fit, glue the parts together and run the template through the planer to clean it up. To align the template and attach the rails, clamp a board into the jig and clamp the guide strip to it (3). Then clamp the rails snug to the top plate below, and screw them to the template.

the workpiece. To attach the rails accurately, clamp an alignment board into the jig, sticking up past the top, and clamp the guide strip tight to the board. Then screw the rails to the template so they fit snugly against the top plate.

Practice with a straight tenon

To get the hang of the jig, I recommend cutting a straight tenon first. Lay out the tenon in pencil, both cheeks and shoulders. Now clamp the workpiece in place, with the top end against the underside of the template. Adjust the template so the guide strip is centered on the layout lines, and then clamp it in place. Last, set the plunge depth on the router so the bottom of the bit lines up with the shoulder line.

Start the router in the raised position and then plunge to full depth without touching the workpiece. Make a light climb cut first, to avoid tearout at the shoulder, and then make conventional cuts to finish the job.

I trim the tenon to width by hand, and it goes quickly. Using a chisel wider than the tenon is thick, I make a shallow chop at the shoulder line, using the pencil line and the existing shoulders to line up the chisel. Then I pare away a small chip (center top photo, facing page). Now I can chop deeper at the shoulder and pare off a longer chip, repeating the process until the tenon is done.

Using the jig for angled tenons. Make a plan view of the seat to figure out the tenon angle, and then make a wedge at that angle, at least 12 in. long. The wedge works on both the tablesaw and the router jig. Start with the ends first. Use the wedge with a miter gauge on the tablesaw to cut off the ends of the workpiece at the correct angle.

Add the wedge. After cutting off a small piece for the back side of the jig, screw the long wedge to the L-fence.

Lay out just one workpiece. Lay out the cheeks and shoulders for one tenon with a sharp pencil. The other tenons need only rough marks to make sure you cut them in the right orientation.

Load in the workpiece. With the workpiece butted against the bottom of the template, clamp it in place. The tip cut from the wedge serves as a clamping block.

Angled tenon is just a wedge away

For angled tenons, I draw a full-size top view of the seat to determine the angle of the tenons, and make a long wedge that will go into the router jig. Make the wedge about the same width as the workpiece, and at least 12 in. long. Cut off a short piece of the wedge to go on the back side of the jig to provide purchase for the clamp.

Before screwing the long wedge in place, use it at the tablesaw to help crosscut the ends of the side seat rails. Now screw the wedge securely to the router jig, clamp a side rail in place, and rout these angled tenons just as you did the straight ones.

Locate the template. Slide it sideways until the guide strip is centered on the tenon layout below.

Rout one side at a time. Plunge the router fully, then start with a light climb cut to prevent tearout at the shoulder. Then make a series of light normal cuts until the guide bushing reaches the guide strip. Now do the same to form the other side of the tenon.

Cut the ends by hand. Use a chisel that is wider than the tenon but narrower than the workpiece to trim the top and bottom of the tenon. Then use a file to round the tenon to match the routed mortises.

Perfect fit on an angled tenon. If the cheeks are a bit fat, trim them with a shoulder or rabbet plane. Then test-fit the tenon and watch the four shoulders close perfectly, with no gaps.

Compound angles are easy, too

For compound-angled tenons, add a second wedge, this one screwed to the jig's fence. Use both wedges together at the tablesaw to cut the end of the rail, then mount them on the jig to rout the tenons.

One last tip: For minor adjustments to the tenons, use tape to shim the jig.

Compound Angle? Add a Second Wedge

On many chairs the seat slopes backward for comfort. On others the back legs are splayed. Do another full-size drawing to determine the angle between the rails and legs.

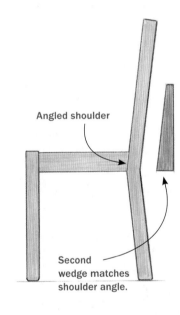

Angled shoulder

Second wedge matches shoulder angle.

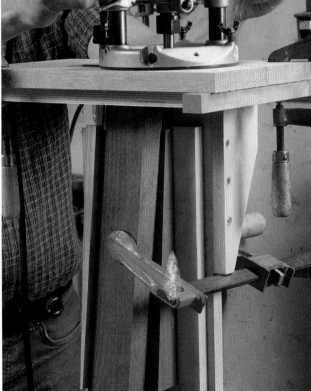

Add the second wedge. The second wedge is screwed to the side of the L-fence (top right), and the two wedges work together to create the compound angle. Mark the parts carefully to be sure you position them correctly in the jig (right) and rout as usual.

PART THREE

PROJECTS

Build a Perfect Picture Frame

MICHAEL CULLEN

When I was starting out in furniture making in the 1980s, some of my first commissions were for picture frames. I made frames mostly for artists, and they appreciated the care I took selecting choice wood, cutting spot-on miters, and reinforcing them with exposed splines. And I really appreciated the commissions—for the money, which I was in dire need of, but also for the opportunity to consolidate some of the fundamental skills I was learning. In the years since then I've built many more frames, tweaking my technique along the way and arriving at solid methods for building strong, understated, elegant frames.

A Basic Molding

Frame stock, ¾ in. thick by 1¼ in. wide

Rabbet, ¼ in. wide by ¾ in. deep, holds artwork package.

Run the rabbet. Two ripcuts on the tablesaw shape the rabbet that will hold the art.

Time for molding. An oval edge bit on the router table produces in one pass the slightly pillowed surface Cullen wants on the front of the frame.

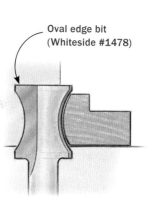

Oval edge bit (Whiteside #1478)

Start with the sled. Before angling the blade, check to be sure the miter gauge is set exactly at 90° to the line of cut.

Tablesaw Sled

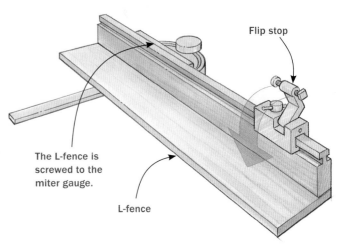

Flip stop

The L-fence is screwed to the miter gauge.

L-fence

Testing, 1, 2 . . . Cullen dials in the blade angle by making test cuts in two extra pieces of frame stock (far left). Using a miter clamp to hold the joint and a framing square to test the resulting angle, Cullen zeros in on the tablesaw blade's tilt angle (left).

Laser focus on the miter

Developing a method for cutting flawless miters without fuss is a key milestone for a furniture maker—and a steady source of pride and pleasure once it's mastered.

Whenever possible, I cut my miters with the tablesaw's blade tilted and the workpiece in a regular crosscut position, either on a sled, a miter gauge, or a sliding table. I think this approach produces a better cut, because the cutting action is less labored and doesn't tend to move the workpiece. It also enables you to use stop blocks more easily, and it works just as well for long workpieces as short ones.

Miter the real molding. Cutting miters with a crosscut setup and a tilted blade makes for clean cuts and easy use of stop blocks. A sacrificial spacer fills the rabbet, stabilizing the workpiece during the cut.

Keep some cutoffs. Cullen uses scraps of the frame stock as clamping blocks, adhering them with glue and finger pressure (above). Just before assembly, they serve as stands while he applies glue to the miters (right).

Pressure in the right place. The clamping blocks enable you to exert pressure perpendicular to the miter joint (above). Be sure they are placed so you can keep the tips of the miters tight. After the glue-up, bandsaw away the bulk of each block (left). Then remove the rest with a handplane.

Sometimes Special Gizmos are Good

To glue up my best frames I use clamping blocks, but if I'm in a hurry or have a batch to do I sometimes reach for my Merle band clamp (mlcswoodworking.com). You just wrap the band around the assembly and tighten. You can't apply pressure directly across the joints or adjust pressure for each corner as you can with clamping blocks, but still it works quite well—and it's hard to beat for speed.

Cutting at exactly 45° is non-negotiable, of course. Some joints might have a little margin for error, but not miters; over time the flaw will tell. To get a perfect 45°, I use scrap stock milled at the same time as the real parts. With a miter clamp to hold the test miters and an accurate framing square to assess the outcome, you can quickly dial in the right blade tilt.

Insert the Splines

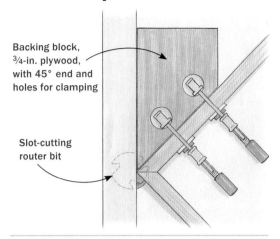

Backing block, ¾-in. plywood, with 45° end and holes for clamping

Slot-cutting router bit

Slotting for the splines. Cullen cuts spline grooves with a slot-cutter at the router table. A piece of scrap stock cut at a 45° angle and drilled to accept clamps guides the frame through the cut.

Spline insertion. The splines, made from the same wood as the frame, are cut so their long grain crosses the miter joint (right). Cullen rough-cuts the excess at the bandsaw (far right), then planes the splines flush.

Splines for strength

Most commercial frames are held together with nails or corrugated fasteners, but if you want to keep solid-wood miters tight for the long term—and give your frame a furniture maker's flourish—I recommend using splines to reinforce the miter joint. I usually cut the grooves for them with a slot-cutter at the router table, which produces a perfectly flat-bottomed kerf. For wide frames that require grooves too deep to cut with the router, I'll use a cradle jig at the tablesaw, then square up the bottom of the groove with a chisel.

Once the splines are glued in, all that remains is the pleasurable task of flushing them off, and your frame is just about ready for art.

Finished frame. Cullen pads on shellac in thin coats, building to a low luster.

Build a Collector's Case

GARY ROGOWSKI

I s it really the devil that's in the details, or is it the angels? In this little collector's case, the details make it stand out. Protruding, shaped dovetail joints, side-hung drawers to keep a low profile, and inlaid pulls all help this piece create a great overall impression.

Even with all the careful touches, the case is simple to construct. Almost all the joints are cut with a router. I use a commercial jig to cut the dovetailed case corners, and I make them stand out with a little handwork.

I built the case and drawers from black walnut. If you need to glue up boards for the case, pay attention to grain and color when you match them up. The drawer fronts should be ripped at the bandsaw from a single board with attractive figure. For the back, I used reclaimed water-tank redwood, which I kept fairly thick. I rabbeted the edges to create a raised panel.

To avoid marring the proud joinery details later, plane, scrape, and lightly sand the case pieces inside and out before starting work on the dovetails.

A jig makes dovetails snug and quick

Naturally, working with a router jig makes quick work of case dovetails, even when it comes to layout. For both tails and pins, you just mark the work and align the jig on the first piece to establish the setup for the remaining cuts.

Begin with the tail boards. Set your router-bit depth to match the thickness of the stock plus the thickness of the template. To this, I added $3/32$ in. for the amount I wanted the joints to protrude. Next, mount the piece in your vise, end grain up, and strike a centerline on the end of the board. Now clamp the straight-fingered jig to the

workpiece, aligning its center with the mark. Last, snug a stop block against the end of the workpiece and clamp it to the jig's wooden cleat. After routing this first set of tails, the block will serve as a reference for locating the jig for all of the remaining tail cuts.

With the dovetail bit installed and set to the proper depth, set the router on top of the template to begin cutting. The bit's guide bearing is sized for an exact fit between the jig's fingers, so guiding the router is straightforward. Take care, though, not to lift the router or you risk damaging the jig.

After cutting the first set of tails, unclamp the jig, flip the board, and secure the jig to cut the tails on the opposite end. Finally, repeat the steps for the second tail board, using the stop block to locate the jig for each set of cuts. After cutting the tails, transfer the locations of a few of them to the pin boards with a sharp pencil. When you clamp the pin template in place, it should be easy to align the jig with these layout lines. If you've attached the jig in the right spot, the fit should be perfect. Install the straight bit in the router and set its depth, remembering the extra $3/32$ in. needed to make the pins stand proud. Take one practice pass before trying it out on your good stock.

The Keller Way of Dovetailing

The Keller jig is a sturdy, flat plate of composite material with two templates, one each for pins and tails. It comes with straight and dovetail bits that are guided by bearings. Attach a clamping cleat of long, square stock, making sure its reference faces are perpendicular to the jig's fingers.

A Case for Details

This simple chest, proportioned to sit atop a desk or dresser, becomes a handsome display piece through smart details: Proud dovetails add depth and character, side-hung drawers show continuous grain across their fronts, and inlaid pulls hint that the drawers contain beautiful things.

FRONT VIEW

18⅛ in.

7¼ in.

2 in.

2 in.

2 in.

¾ in.

¾ in.

2 in.

SIDE VIEW

11½ in.

8 in.

12¼ in.

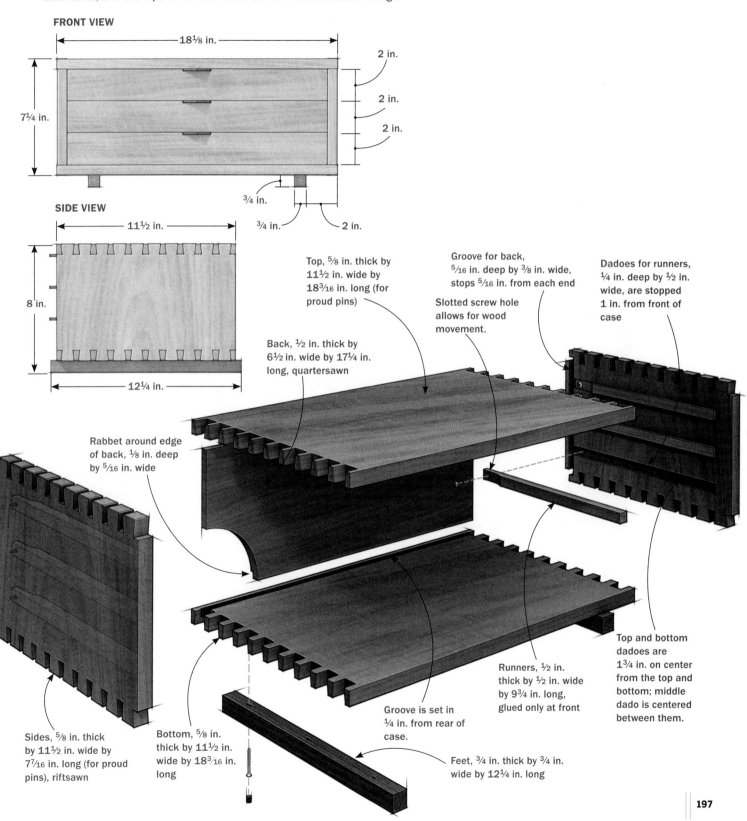

Top, ⅝ in. thick by 11½ in. wide by 18³⁄₁₆ in. long (for proud pins)

Back, ½ in. thick by 6½ in. wide by 17¼ in. long, quartersawn

Groove for back, ⁵⁄₁₆ in. deep by ⅜ in. wide, stops ⁵⁄₁₆ in. from each end

Slotted screw hole allows for wood movement.

Dadoes for runners, ¼ in. deep by ½ in. wide, are stopped 1 in. from front of case

Rabbet around edge of back, ⅛ in. deep by ⁵⁄₁₆ in. wide

Sides, ⅝ in. thick by 11½ in. wide by 7⁷⁄₁₆ in. long (for proud pins), riftsawn

Bottom, ⅝ in. thick by 11½ in. wide by 18³⁄₁₆ in. long

Groove is set in ¼ in. from rear of case.

Runners, ½ in. thick by ½ in. wide by 9¾ in. long, glued only at front

Top and bottom dadoes are 1¾ in. on center from the top and bottom; middle dado is centered between them.

Feet, ¾ in. thick by ¾ in. wide by 12¼ in. long

Set up and cut the tails first. After marking a centerline (top) and aligning
the template (above left), clamp the jig in place and cut the tails (above right).
The stop block clamped to the cleat helps locate the jig for the remaining cuts.

Transfer the layout. Carefully scribe several tails onto the pin board to help locate the jig (top). Align the jig so that the edges of the fingers are tight against the scribe lines (above). Then rout the pins (right).

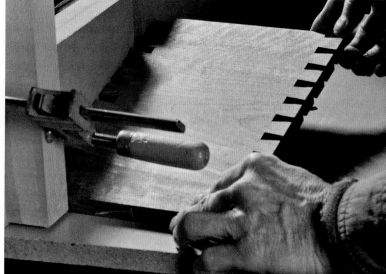

Dadoes hold the drawer runners. Each cut is stopped at both ends, so limit the travel of the workpiece with blocks on the infeed and outfeed fences. Start the cut with the piece against the infeed stop and slowly lower the work onto the spinning bit. Set the bit to the cut's full depth but use a hardboard shim on the tabletop to enable a shallow first pass.

Outfit the interior before gluing up

The side-hung drawers slide on runners attached to the case sides. I seat these runners in stopped dadoes cut at the router table before gluing up the case. The front of the dado stops 1 in. from the front edge of the case and ⅝ in. from the rear, where it intersects with the groove for the back. Clamp a pair of stop blocks to the router table's fence, and make the ¼-in.-deep cuts using a ½-in. straight bit (photo, p. 199, bottom right). Afterward, use a marking gauge to scribe the end lines at the front and then square them with a chisel.

Cut the stopped grooves for the back next. I make them 5⁄16 in. deep, and I make the rabbet cut into the back the same size.

Mill up the drawer runners slightly oversize, then plane each one for a snug fit in the dado. To allow for cross-grain movement with the sides, I glue only the front 2 in. of each runner, attaching the rear with a screw in a slotted hole.

Square up. Scribe a line to mark the front end of each dado, then use a chisel to chop the routed ends square.

Install the runners. To account for wood movement, Rogowski glues only the first 2 in. of the runner and secures the rear with a screw in a slotted hole.

With the runners installed, chamfer the proud ends of the dovetails with a block plane and chisel, and dry-fit the case. As a last step prior to glue-up, I prefinish the case pieces, inside and out, with shellac. To avoid squeeze-out, I paint the glue carefully on each pin using a narrow piece of veneer. Start by gluing the top and bottom to one side, then drop the back into position and glue up the remaining side. Secure the whole assembly with two clamps each along the top and bottom of the case. Protect the case sides from dents with cauls set just inside the joinery.

Prepare for glue-up. Lightly chamfer the ends of the pins and tails (top), and apply finish to all surfaces that won't receive glue, including the end grain on the tails (above).

Glue up the case. Slide the rabbeted back into place after attaching the top and bottom to the first side.

Assemble the drawers

The drawer boxes go together easily. Grooves cut into the drawer sides allow them to slide on the case-mounted runners. I make the bottoms from plywood and line them with velvet over a layer of acid-free mat board.

Start by cutting the drawer fronts to exact length. Adjust them to the case by handplaning to fit with a low-angle plane. The fit should be tight. Size the height of each front so that all three drawers can fit into the opening at once, but just barely.

To join the drawer fronts and backs to the sides, I use an easy-to-assemble rabbeted dovetail joint that can be cut quickly on the router table (photos, facing page). I start with the fronts and backs, using the tablesaw first to cut away the bulk of the waste from the rabbet. Then, at the router table, I make a light cut with the dovetail bit to give the rabbet its angled cheek.

For the drawer sides, leave the bit depth unchanged and use test cuts to adjust the fence setting for a proper cut. You want the drawer side just proud of the front when the joint comes together (photos, facing page). You'll plane it flush later.

To maximize storage space in the shallow drawers, I screw the plywood bottoms into rabbets rather than setting them into a groove. Cut the rabbets at the router table and then glue up each drawer. I reinforce and decorate each corner joint with maple pins.

To rout the stopped grooves for the drawer runners, use a setup piece milled to the same width as a drawer side. Position the scrap inside the case and mark it with the location of the runner. Make test cuts until you cut a groove that fits the runner with just a touch of up-and-down play. Now you're ready to groove the real drawers. Set the stop on the fence to cut each groove a little short at the

Build and Fit the Drawers

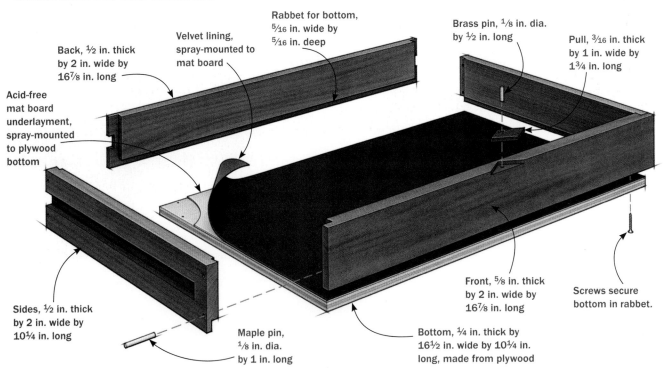

Back, ½ in. thick by 2 in. wide by 16⅞ in. long

Velvet lining, spray-mounted to mat board

Rabbet for bottom, 5/16 in. wide by 5/16 in. deep

Brass pin, ⅛ in. dia. by ½ in. long

Pull, 3/16 in. thick by 1 in. wide by 1¾ in. long

Acid-free mat board underlayment, spray-mounted to plywood bottom

Sides, ½ in. thick by 2 in. wide by 10¼ in. long

Maple pin, ⅛ in. dia. by 1 in. long

Front, ⅝ in. thick by 2 in. wide by 16⅞ in. long

Screws secure bottom in rabbet.

Bottom, ¼ in. thick by 16½ in. wide by 10¼ in. long, made from plywood

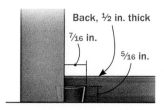

Rabbet the front and back.
With most of the waste removed at the tablesaw, Rogowski shapes the rabbet at the router table using a dovetail bit.

Back, ½ in. thick
⁷⁄₁₆ in.
⁵⁄₁₆ in.

front end. Also, leave the bit depth shallow at first and adjust using multiple cuts until the drawer just slides in. Use a chisel to square the stopped ends of the grooves. Handplane the faces of the drawer sides until they slide sweetly on their runners. Then plane the top and bottom edges of the drawer to adjust the gaps between drawers. Finally, plane the drawer fronts as needed to bring them flush with one another.

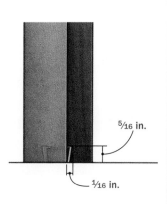

⁵⁄₁₆ in.
¹⁄₁₆ in.

Cut a half tail on the drawer side. Adjust the fence for a light cut and run the stock vertically past the bit. Leave the bit height unchanged to match the depth of the rabbet.

Test the fit. Your half-tail should be shallower than the one on this test cut, so the drawer side stands just proud of the end grain of the front.

Glue up the drawers. Use cauls, apply even clamping pressure, and check for square.

Reinforce the joinery. To add strength and a decorative touch, Rogowski seats two pins made from maple through the drawer side at each corner.

Rout the runner grooves. Make them in two passes, shimming the fence for the first pass. Aim for a tight fit.

Fit the drawers. Plane the faces of each drawer side until the drawer slides smoothly into its opening. Then plane the bottom edges of the drawer sides and the top and bottom edges of the drawer fronts, to adjust the gaps between the drawers.

Make and attach the pulls

The final touch is to inlay the pulls. I cut the diamond shape on the tablesaw using an angled stop block and a hold-down stick. I cut all the pulls, sand or plane them to shape, and then scribe the shape on each drawer front. I rout the insets and clean up the corners with a sharp chisel. Glue and clamp the pulls in place. After they've dried, add a small brass pin to each pull.

Beautiful Bandsawn Boxes

MICHAEL CULLEN

Ibuild a lot of furniture—often complex, exacting pieces carefully mapped out in scale drawings. Some years ago I began making bandsawn boxes as a way to relieve the tension of working on such long, demanding projects. The boxes are quick, requiring no measuring, no joinery, and almost no planning. They welcome creativity, opening a door to limitless variations of form and embellishment. And most of all, they are fun. I can grab a piece of scrap, make a fast pencil sketch right on the wood, and work freehand at the bandsaw to create a box in no time.

I've always admired Shaker boxes, with their combination of good form and minimal material making a container that is lightweight, strong, and elegant. My goal with bandsawn boxes is similar: to push the limits of the material without compromising strength or function—and wind up with something beautiful.

I cut the boxes from a single chunk of wood, sawing it apart and then gluing it right back together with some parts removed. This makes for perfect grain matches and no issues of wood movement. I cut a tapered plug from the center of the blank, which I use to make a perfectly fitting bottom to the box as well as a keeper that holds the lid in place.

I make two types of bandsawn boxes. One has two curved walls that meet in a point at each end. The other is a four-walled, rectangular form. Almost all the steps for making the two types are the same.

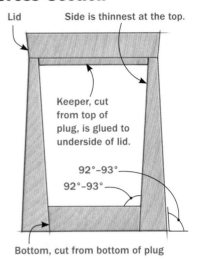

Lid   Side is thinnest at the top.

Keeper, cut from top of plug, is glued to underside of lid.

92°–93°
92°–93°

Bottom, cut from bottom of plug

Two-walled box

To make the two-walled box, start with a thick block of wood: 12/4 or 16/4 stock is optimal. Some of my favorite species for bandsawn boxes are basswood, walnut, mahogany, maple, and cherry. I carve and milk-paint many of my boxes, but I leave some unadorned.

Flatten the top and bottom of the blank, making the surfaces parallel. The sides don't have to be milled, but the glue-up will be easier if they are not too uneven. There's no required size for a blank, but one about 8 in. long by 4 in. wide by 3 in. or 4 in. tall would be good for a first try.

The first step at the bandsaw is to cut the lid from the block. Then set the lid blank aside and draw the shape of the box on the top of the box blank. These lines will define the interior of the box, so be sure to leave space outside the lines for the wall thickness.

To saw out the interior, angle the bandsaw table roughly 3° off horizontal. A little more or less is fine. The idea is to make the interior cavity tapered—smaller at the bottom—so the tapered plug can be used to make a perfectly fitting box bottom. Saw steadily without rushing, so the blade tracks without deflection. The better the cut, the better the

The First Two Cuts

Make the two cuts in opposing directions to yield a tapered plug.

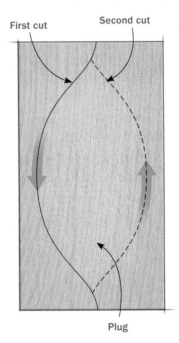

First cut   Second cut

Plug

joints will be. I use a ¼-in. blade with 4 or 6 tpi (teeth per inch). With the cuts complete, bring the outer halves together. The joints at each end should mate with no light showing through.

Initial sawing. After milling a block of wood, saw a slice off the top and set it aside—this will become the lid.

Glue up the sides (photo, p. 208, top left), and when the glue has cured, drop in the plug. It should rest slightly below the bottom of the sides and form a perfect seal. Mark the plug where it emerges, then remove it and draw a second line at least ¼ in. above the first. With the bandsaw table still angled, cut along both lines to create the box bottom. Take a slice off the top of the plug to make the keeper for the lid.

Cutting the outside perimeter of the box is easy: Use a pencil with one finger held against the inside surface of the box and trace around the cavity, then cut to the line. Walls that are too thick make a box look clumsy; I typically make them about ⅛ in. thick at the top, which gives a light, graceful feeling. For a wall that is thicker at the bottom, creating a solid look as on this box, you can leave the bandsaw table at the same tilt as for the inside wall but approach the cut from the opposite direction.

Tilt the table. After cutting off the lid, Cullen creates the interior cavity of the box by cutting a tapered plug from the blank. Set the bandsaw table a few degrees off horizontal before cutting out the plug.

Two curving cuts. For a box with pointed ends, two sawcuts are all it takes to shape the interior walls. Cullen makes a shallow test cut into the end grain to confirm that the blade is angled in the right direction and will yield a cavity that is smaller at the bottom.

Glue up the sides. Don't overdo the glue. Apply it carefully to prevent squeeze-out inside the box, where it is very difficult to clean up.

Hands before clamps. To be sure the bandsawn joints line up perfectly, fit the halves together first with hand pressure. Hold them firmly together for a minute or two to let the glue get tacky before applying clamps.

Slice the plug. To create the perfectly fitting bottom of the box, first push the plug into the cavity and draw a line around it where it emerges.

Two cuts to get the bottom. With the bandsaw table still angled, saw off the waste piece at the lower end of the plug, then take a second slice to make the bottom of the box. Last, cut a slice off the top of the plug—this will be the keeper on the underside of the lid.

Take Three Slices from the Plug

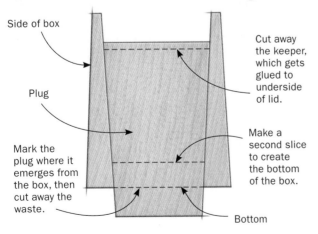

Side of box

Cut away the keeper, which gets glued to underside of lid.

Plug

Make a second slice to create the bottom of the box.

Mark the plug where it emerges from the box, then cut away the waste.

Bottom

After gluing the lid keeper to the lid blank, put the lid on the box and trace the outside shape of the box on the underside of the lid. Then cut out the lid. I often make the cut so the lid flares outward. It looks good and makes the lid easier to grip. I usually fair the curves and smooth the bandsawn texture with rasps and files, and finish with sandpaper on a flat sanding block, beginning at 100 grit and ending with 400. For more aggressive shaping, I'll use the disk sander.

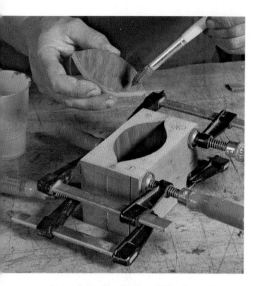

Complete the body of the box. If you'd like to paint the inside of the box, now is the time, while you have access from top and bottom. Paint the bottom as well.

Free the box from the blank. To create walls that are thicker at the bottom, leave the table tilted as before but approach the cut from the opposite direction.

Pop in the bottom. After brushing a narrow band of glue around the lowest part of the inside walls, drop the bottom into the cavity and press it into place.

Add the lid. Guided by a tracing of the inside of the box cavity, Cullen glues the keeper to the underside of the lid blank. He presses the keeper into place, holds it a minute, then clamps it.

Sizing the lid. After gluing on the keeper, fit the inverted box onto it and trace the perimeter of the box onto the lid blank. Then remove the box and saw out the lid.

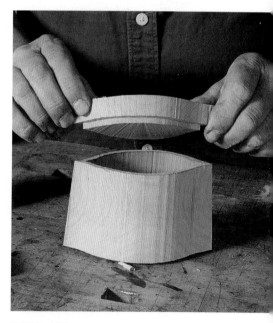

A fitting lid. Cullen saws the lid at an angle opposite to the walls of the box. The flare looks good and also makes the lid easier to lift off.

Take Four Slices

1. To establish the interior of the box, first make two slices lengthwise.

Plug

2. Then crosscut.

92°–93°

Four-walled box

To make a four-walled bandsawn box, you'll follow nearly every step of the procedure for a two-walled box. The only real difference is in the pattern of cuts you'll make to the box blank once you've sliced off the lid blank.

After slicing off the lid blank, draw the design directly on the top of the box blank. Again, you'll want the interior cavity to taper inward from top to bottom, so angle the bandsaw table a few degrees. Slice lengthwise through the block for the first cut, then the second. The blank will now be three long, narrow pieces. It's a good idea to mark them so they'll go back together in the correct order. Now crosscut the central piece at each end to define the ends of the box's interior.

The glue-up here is slightly trickier than for a two-walled box. To keep the parts aligned during assembly, I often do the glue-up around the plug. Be careful when applying glue to avoid squeeze-out, which could glue the plug in place.

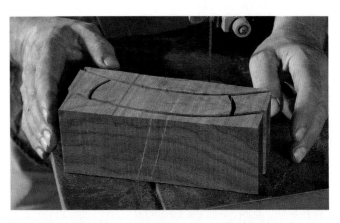

From a blank to a box. With the bandsaw table angled a few degrees, make the two long cuts first, then the short ones to create a four-walled box.

Assemble around the plug. Cullen uses the plug to help keep the parts positioned for gluing. Careful glue application and the kerf spaces at either end of the plug keep it from getting glued into the box.

Plug yields more boxes. Cullen often uses the plug from one bandsawn box to make a smaller nesting box. The plug he's holding (below) yielded two more boxes (right).

Saw the outside walls. After glue-up, cut the outside walls to free the box from the blank.

Saddled lid

The lids of these bandsawn boxes are open to all sorts of variations. The box and its lid can be flat-topped, scooped, crowned, and even wildly undulating. I made the lid for the mahogany box on p. 212 so it curves downward in the middle. The process tracks the steps for making a flat lid with just a couple of exceptions.

When I cut the lid blank from the box blank, I simply drew a curved line and followed it. Had I drawn a squiggly line, the lid would fit just as well. After cutting out the sides of the box, I sliced the lid keeper from the top of the plug, cutting parallel to the curving top face of the plug. I glued the keeper to the lid blank while the lid blank was still flat on top. Then I sawed the top of the lid to a parallel curve. I could just as easily have left it flat on top or sawn it to a wavy surface. Experimentation is the name of the bandsaw boxmaker's game.

Cut a Curved Lid

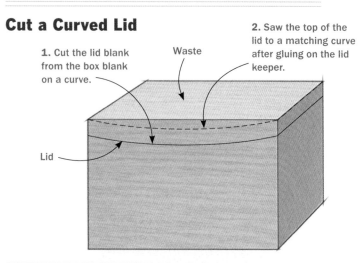

1. Cut the lid blank from the box blank on a curve.

Waste

2. Saw the top of the lid to a matching curve after gluing on the lid keeper.

Lid

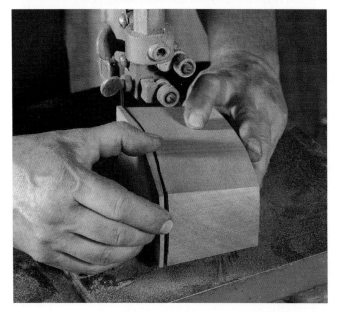

Cut away the lid on a curve. To make a lid that's dished end to end, cut the lid from the box blank on a curving line (top). After cutting the box apart, slice the keeper from the top of the plug, following a parallel curve (above).

Press the keeper into place. After applying glue—be careful to stay well inside the perimeter line—press the keeper onto the lid blank and hold it a minute (top). Then add clamps and use the plug, which is sawn to the identical curve, as a custom caul. With the keeper glued in place, saw the top of the lid to a mating curve (above).

Elegant Bookcase from Top to Bottom

MIKE KORSAK

If you read and appreciate books, as I do, then you probably appreciate the functional aspects of a bookcase. If you enjoy beautiful materials and elegant, understated design, as I do, then I hope the design of this piece will appeal to you as well. I built it with a matched set of curly maple boards, which I purchased from Irion Lumber. I paired the maple with sexy, straight-grained bubinga for the base. And I used East Indian rosewood as an accent.

Bookcase with Drawers

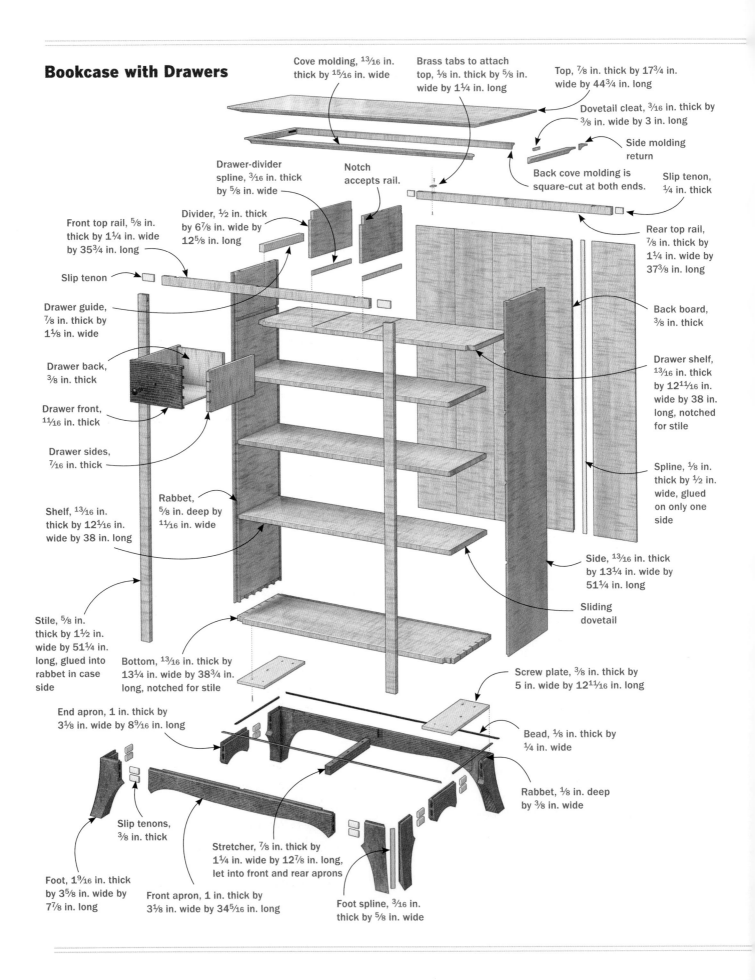

Cove molding, $^{13}/_{16}$ in. thick by $^{15}/_{16}$ in. wide

Brass tabs to attach top, $^{1}/_{8}$ in. thick by $^{5}/_{8}$ in. wide by $1^{1}/_{4}$ in. long

Top, $^{7}/_{8}$ in. thick by $17^{3}/_{4}$ in. wide by $44^{3}/_{4}$ in. long

Dovetail cleat, $^{3}/_{16}$ in. thick by $^{3}/_{8}$ in. wide by 3 in. long

Side molding return

Drawer-divider spline, $^{3}/_{16}$ in. thick by $^{5}/_{8}$ in. wide

Notch accepts rail.

Back cove molding is square-cut at both ends.

Slip tenon, $^{1}/_{4}$ in. thick

Front top rail, $^{5}/_{8}$ in. thick by $1^{1}/_{4}$ in. wide by $35^{3}/_{4}$ in. long

Divider, $^{1}/_{2}$ in. thick by $6^{7}/_{8}$ in. wide by $12^{5}/_{8}$ in. long

Rear top rail, $^{7}/_{8}$ in. thick by $1^{1}/_{4}$ in. wide by $37^{3}/_{8}$ in. long

Slip tenon

Drawer guide, $^{7}/_{8}$ in. thick by $1^{1}/_{8}$ in. wide

Back board, $^{3}/_{8}$ in. thick

Drawer back, $^{3}/_{8}$ in. thick

Drawer shelf, $^{13}/_{16}$ in. thick by $12^{11}/_{16}$ in. wide by 38 in. long, notched for stile

Drawer front, $^{11}/_{16}$ in. thick

Drawer sides, $^{7}/_{16}$ in. thick

Spline, $^{1}/_{8}$ in. thick by $^{1}/_{2}$ in. wide, glued on only one side

Shelf, $^{13}/_{16}$ in. thick by $12^{1}/_{16}$ in. wide by 38 in. long

Rabbet, $^{5}/_{8}$ in. deep by $^{11}/_{16}$ in. wide

Side, $^{13}/_{16}$ in. thick by $13^{1}/_{4}$ in. wide by $51^{1}/_{4}$ in. long

Sliding dovetail

Stile, $^{5}/_{8}$ in. thick by $1^{1}/_{2}$ in. wide by $51^{1}/_{4}$ in. long, glued into rabbet in case side

Bottom, $^{13}/_{16}$ in. thick by $13^{1}/_{4}$ in. wide by $38^{3}/_{4}$ in. long, notched for stile

Screw plate, $^{3}/_{8}$ in. thick by 5 in. wide by $12^{11}/_{16}$ in. long

End apron, 1 in. thick by $3^{1}/_{8}$ in. wide by $8^{9}/_{16}$ in. long

Bead, $^{1}/_{8}$ in. thick by $^{1}/_{4}$ in. wide

Rabbet, $^{1}/_{8}$ in. deep by $^{3}/_{8}$ in. wide

Slip tenons, $^{3}/_{8}$ in. thick

Stretcher, $^{7}/_{8}$ in. thick by $1^{1}/_{4}$ in. wide by $12^{7}/_{8}$ in. long, let into front and rear aprons

Foot, $1^{9}/_{16}$ in. thick by $3^{5}/_{8}$ in. wide by $7^{7}/_{8}$ in. long

Front apron, 1 in. thick by $3^{1}/_{8}$ in. wide by $34^{5}/_{16}$ in. long

Foot spline, $^{3}/_{16}$ in. thick by $^{5}/_{8}$ in. wide

FRONT VIEW

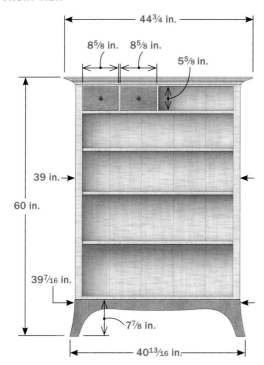

44¾ in.

8⅝ in.   8⅝ in.

5⅝ in.

60 in.

39 in.

39⁷⁄₁₆ in.

7⅞ in.

40¹³⁄₁₆ in.

TOP/MOLDING DETAIL

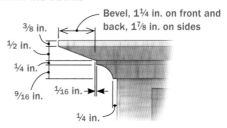

Bevel, 1¼ in. on front and back, 1⅞ in. on sides

⅜ in.

½ in.

¼ in.

⁹⁄₁₆ in.

¹⁄₁₆ in.

¼ in.

There is a lot of exacting joinery in the carcase, which has sliding dovetails joining the shelves to the sides and half-blind dovetails joining the sides to the bottom. That's all spelled out in the drawing. But for this article I've chosen to focus on the base and the top molding. These two components might not be the first things to catch your eye, but they are vital to the look of the piece, and they are both a bit more challenging than they might seem.

Feet first

The feet on this base pack a lot of curves and unusual joinery into a small space. I begin making them by cutting the angled kerf for the gunstock miters. These little miters add a bit of refinement to the design and also eliminate short grain that might be prone to breaking off. I cut them with a miter gauge on the tablesaw. I cut the mating miters on the aprons now as well.

With those cut, I mortise the feet and aprons to accept slip tenons. I do this with a plunge router and a ⅜-in. upcutting end mill bit. I built a jig for the router that makes the mortising go quite smoothly.

The feet flare outward, making the feet and aprons slightly concave on their outer faces. To create that flare, I make a curved

SIDE VIEW

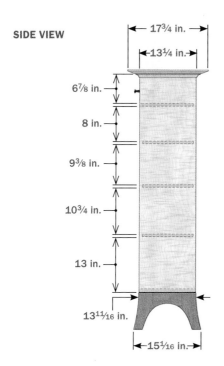

17¾ in.

13¼ in.

6⅞ in.

8 in.

9⅜ in.

10¾ in.

13 in.

13¹¹⁄₁₆ in.

15¹⁄₁₆ in.

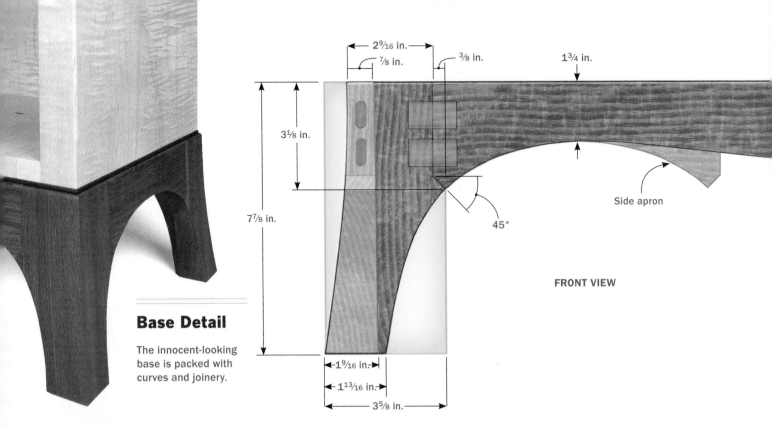

2⁹⁄₁₆ in.
⁷⁄₈ in.
³⁄₈ in.
1³⁄₄ in.

3¹⁄₈ in.

7⁷⁄₈ in.

Side apron

45°

FRONT VIEW

Base Detail

The innocent-looking base is packed with curves and joinery.

1⁹⁄₁₆ in.
1¹³⁄₁₆ in.
3⁵⁄₈ in.

Canted kerf. The base joinery begins with a kerf cut in the foot blank at 45° for the gunstock miter.

Sliding jig for slip tenons. Korsak made a router jig that has a channel on the back that captures the router fence, steadying the cut.

Bandsaw the sweep. The face of the foot is bandsawn to a curve.

The feet meet in a miter. Korsak miters the feet at the tablesaw, cutting in several passes to reduce pressure on the short workpiece.

Slot for a spline. With the feet mitered and the fence moved to the other side of the blade, cut a groove for the spline.

Finish the gunstock. Korsak roughs out the shoulder on the bandsaw. He'll follow up with multiple crosscuts on the tablesaw.

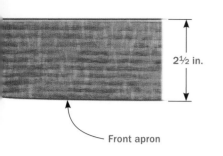

Front apron

2½ in.

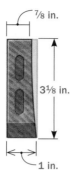

⅞ in.

3⅛ in.

1 in.

BASE END VIEW

Nibble to a curve. Korsak creates the slight concavity on the outer face of the apron with multiple passes at the tablesaw, adjusting the fence and the blade height with each pass.

Complete the sweep. Having left some wood at the edge of the apron to support it as he cut the sweep, Korsak flips the board on edge to cut that wood away.

template and trace it onto the feet. Then I use the bandsaw to cut the profile. I'll remove some of the bandsaw marks at this point with hand tools, but I wait until the base is fully assembled to finish the cleanup.

Next I cut the miters where the two halves of each foot are joined. I rip these miters on the tablesaw, with the blade set at 45°. Then, without changing the sawblade angle, I move the fence to the opposite side of the blade and cut spline grooves in the mitered faces.

Finish the joinery by bandsawing away the material above the gunstock miters. These cuts can be cleaned up using a crosscut sled at the tablesaw by nibbling across, taking multiple passes. Do final fitting with a block plane and chisel.

At this point I rough out the concave face of the aprons. First I dry-assemble each foot-to-apron joint and trace the curve of the foot onto the end grain of the apron. Then, at the tablesaw, I make multiple ripcuts to waste the bulk of the wood. Afterward, to fair the curve, I use a spokeshave with a convex sole.

Before moving on to assembly, I bandsaw the curved cutout along the edges of the feet and aprons. I leave a little extra material at the gunstock miter, where the transition from foot to apron occurs. I'll clean this up after assembly.

Cut the edge of the apron. Using relief cuts and entering from both ends in turn, Korsak carefully cuts out the curved edge of the apron.

Finish shaping the foot. With the sweep and the miter cut, bandsaw the foot's curved edge. It will get cleaned up after assembly.

Assembling the base

Base assembly begins with gluing the foot-to-apron joints one at a time. After the subassemblies are glued up, I use a handplane to flush the tops of the feet to the tops of the aprons and to ensure that the tops of the subassemblies are flat. I also mill a rabbet on the top to accept the decorative rosewood bead that punctuates the transition from base to case.

I take the time now to fine-tune the fit of the foot miters, using a block plane and dry-fitting each joint. With each joint dialed in,

I preglue a spline into one of the feet at each corner joint. This saves valuable time during the glue-up and ensures that the spline won't shift and prevent the joint from pulling together properly.

To help with the final glue-ups, I make custom clamping cauls using offcuts generated while making the feet. Each caul is made with two offcuts—one matching the concave face of the foot and one matching the curved edge. To those two pieces I add a block ripped at 45°, which lets me exert clamping pressure perpendicular to the miter joint. With so much attention on preparation, actually gluing the corner joints is fairly straightforward. I tackle them one at a time.

Beads make everything better

Before attaching the base to the carcase, make and install the rosewood bead. I shape the bead with a scratch stock, working on both edges of a wide blank. Then I rip them off the blank at the bandsaw and refine the bead with files and sandpaper. If I don't have

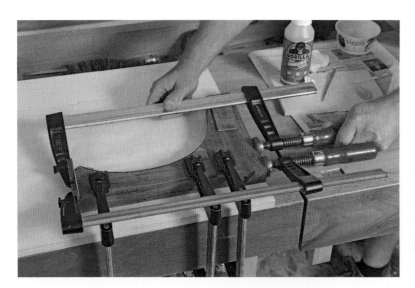

One foot at a time. Using a mitered cutoff as a caul to protect its vulnerable mitered edge, Korsak glues the foot to the apron.

Interrupt the assembly. After gluing feet to both ends of each apron, cut the rabbet where the decorative bead will be seated.

Excellent caul. Using cutoffs from shaping the foot, Korsak makes clamping cauls that fit its face and edge curves and enable him to exert pressure perpendicular to the miter joint.

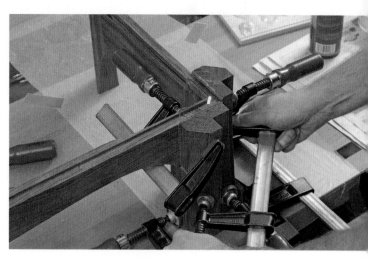

Careful at the corners. Korsak glues up one corner of the base at a time for maximum control. For the last corner he separates the feet just enough to apply glue to the miter and spline.

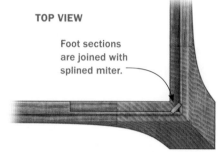

TOP VIEW

Foot sections are joined with splined miter.

Beads by hand. With a shopmade scratch stock, Korsak cuts beads on both edges of a wide rosewood workpiece.

stock long enough for the longest runs, I scarf shorter beads end to end.

I thoroughly enjoy installing the beads. Working with hand tools to cut and fit the miter and scarf joints is almost meditative, and the results are extremely rewarding. I drill pilot holes in the bead to prevent splitting, add a small amount of PVA glue, and fasten the bead with brads. I use glue sparingly, because squeeze-out around a bead can be difficult to remove.

Slit into strips. Cut the beads free at the bandsaw, then smooth the bandsawn face of the bead with a handplane.

Create the cove molding

Now it's on to the cove molding. I use blanks wide enough to yield two pieces of molding and shape the cove on the router table. To achieve a slightly elliptical cove with a round core box bit, I nibble to the layout line by adjusting the bit depth and fence location for each pass. This leaves a ribbed profile, which I clean up with a curved card scraper followed by sandpaper. Then I rip the moldings to width.

The carcase is designed so the sides can expand and contract with the seasons. The cove moldings on the case sides have to permit this movement, so I fix them at the front end with screws and glue, but attach them at the back with sliding-dovetail cleats.

With my molding stock made, I miter both ends of the front piece and screw it in place from inside the case. Then I cut and fit the mating miters on the front ends of the side molding pieces. I leave the back ends of the side moldings long for now. Next I mill a stopped dovetail socket in the back end of each side molding piece on the router table. I also mill a socket in a length of scrap molding.

To make the cleat stock, I reset the router fence and creep up on the size, using scrap molding to check the fit. Then I rip the cleats off the blank and cut them to about 3 in. To help install the cleats, I use the same piece

Glue the beads into the rabbet. Korsak uses painter's tape to keep the beads in place as he fixes them with glue and brads.

Screws keep the base in place. Elongated clearance holes permit the case to move with the seasons.

Mount the Cove Molding

Side moldings are screwed and glued at the front end but unglued at the back; the dovetail cleat holds them tight but lets the case side expand and contract with the seasons.

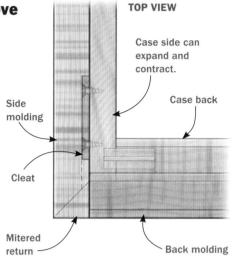

TOP VIEW

Case side can expand and contract.

Side molding

Case back

Cleat

Mitered return

Back molding

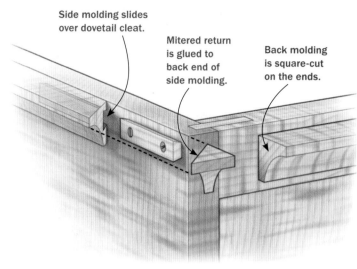

Side molding slides over dovetail cleat.

Mitered return is glued to back end of side molding.

Back molding is square-cut on the ends.

Mitered molding. Having routed and scraped the cove molding to shape, Korsak miters it at the tablesaw. He keeps extra molding for setup later.

A socket in the back. Korsak routs a stopped socket in the back of the side molding to accept the dovetail cleat.

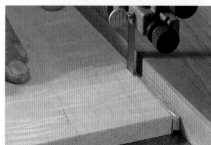

Cleat making. With the dovetail bit at the same height as for the socket, create cleat stock on an oversize blank (above left). Korsak routs the cleat to a tight fit, then adjusts it with a plane. When the fit of the cleat is right, cut it off at the bandsaw (top and above).

Invaluable scrap. A piece of scrap molding with a dovetail socket guides attachment of the cleat. Clamp the scrap flush to the top of the case, slide the cleat into the socket, and drill and screw it into place.

Slide on the side molding. Having already cut and fit the front miters on the side molding, Korsak unscrews the front molding and slides the side molding onto the cleat to mark for the rear miters.

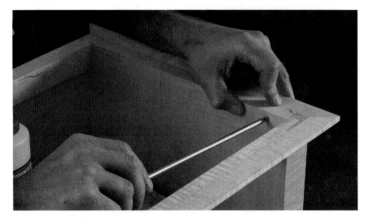

Fixed at the front. The side molding is screwed and glued at the front end but not at the back, where it is held tight to the case by the cleat.

Tiny return. Because of the seasonal movement of the case sides, the side molding can't be joined to the back molding. For a clean seam Korsak glues tiny mitered returns to the back end of the side molding.

of scrap molding. Cut to about 4 in. long, notched and drilled with two access holes, this scrap is now a jig for locating, drilling out, and screwing in the cleats.

With the cleats installed, unscrew the front molding, slide the side moldings onto the cleats, and then reattach the front molding. Check the fit of the miters, then mark the back ends of the side moldings for length. After cutting the back miters and reinstalling the moldings, glue on a mitered return at the back end. This will mate with (but not be joined to) the back molding. Once the cove molding is complete, attach the top.

Finished piece. With the cove molding complete, Korsak attaches the top of the case.

A Fresh Take on the Trestle Table

MARCUS SOTO

As the design and production partner at New York Heartwoods, I set out to create furniture that looked elegant and handcrafted yet for business purposes had to be quick to build and simple to repeat. This trestle-style table is the perfect example. The top is a gorgeous slab of 6/4 book-matched eastern black walnut. I didn't want to distract from the beauty of that wood, so I designed a restrained, rectilinear base that complements the natural beauty of the top. The base joinery consists of half laps and bridle joints, with slight angles and tapers, and optional pegs to add interest.

Trestle table

Soto pairs the natural beauty of a book-matched, live-edge top with a subtle base, adding new twists with the joinery and angle details.

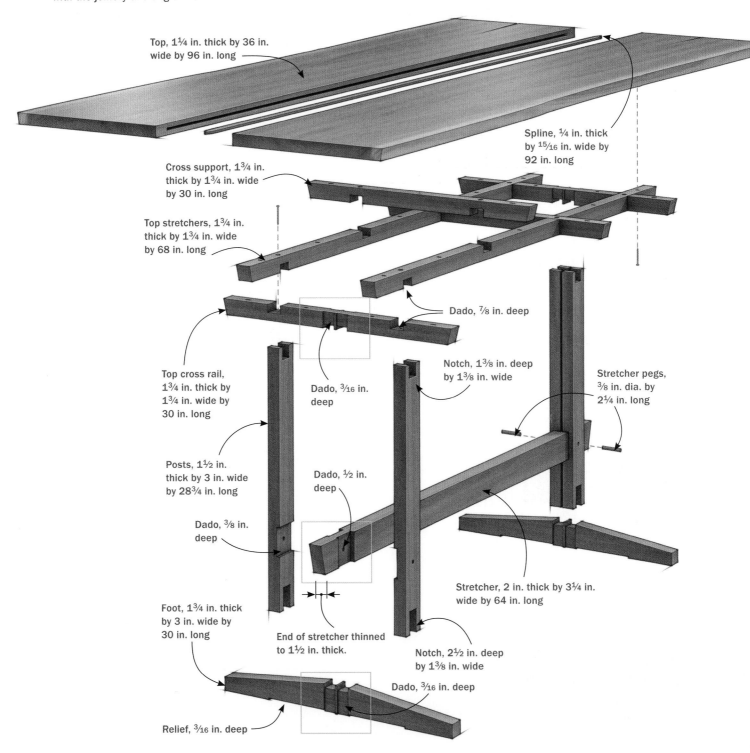

Top, 1¼ in. thick by 36 in. wide by 96 in. long

Spline, ¼ in. thick by 15/16 in. wide by 92 in. long

Cross support, 1¾ in. thick by 1¾ in. wide by 30 in. long

Top stretchers, 1¾ in. thick by 1¾ in. wide by 68 in. long

Dado, 7/8 in. deep

Top cross rail, 1¾ in. thick by 1¾ in. wide by 30 in. long

Dado, 3/16 in. deep

Notch, 1⅜ in. deep by 1⅜ in. wide

Stretcher pegs, ⅜ in. dia. by 2¼ in. long

Posts, 1½ in. thick by 3 in. wide by 28¾ in. long

Dado, ½ in. deep

Dado, ⅜ in. deep

Stretcher, 2 in. thick by 3¼ in. wide by 64 in. long

Foot, 1¾ in. thick by 3 in. wide by 30 in. long

End of stretcher thinned to 1½ in. thick.

Notch, 2½ in. deep by 1⅜ in. wide

Dado, 3/16 in. deep

Relief, 3/16 in. deep

SIDE VIEW

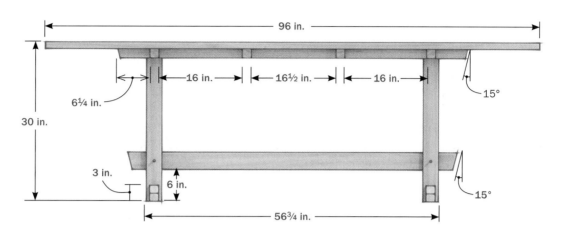

96 in.

6¼ in.

16 in. — 16½ in. — 16 in.

15°

30 in.

3 in.

6 in.

15°

56¾ in.

JOINERY DETAILS

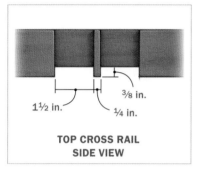

1½ in.

¼ in.

⅜ in.

**TOP CROSS RAIL
SIDE VIEW**

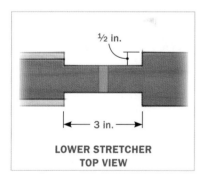

½ in.

3 in.

**LOWER STRETCHER
TOP VIEW**

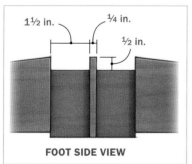

1½ in.

¼ in.

½ in.

FOOT SIDE VIEW

END VIEW

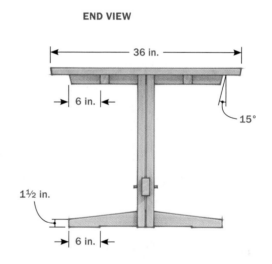

36 in.

6 in.

15°

1½ in.

6 in.

Feet and rails come first

Although the top is the focal point of the piece, construction starts with the base. To begin, lay out the joinery for the feet and the top cross rails. These pieces are the same length, which simplifies layout and reduces setup time. The cross rails and the feet each have two bridle joints separated by a ¼-in. strip in the middle. This creates an interesting visual break between the posts without sacrificing strength and rigidity.

I cut the dadoes in the top cross rails and feet at the same time using a tablesaw and a series of stops. First cut the dadoes on both sides of the cross rails and around the feet. Next, raise the dado blade and cut the deeper dadoes on the top of the feet and the bottom of the cross rails. These deeper dadoes lock in the bridle joint and create more purchase.

The spacer strips on the cross rails and feet are vulnerable short-grain pieces and are not strictly necessary. Personally, I leave the strips, but I make certain to use caution during dry-fittings and glue-ups to avoid snapping them off.

Cut a bridle joint on the feet and top cross rails.
Using a dado set, establish one shoulder of the joint by registering on the fence (left). Then slide the piece to register on the stop, cut the other shoulder, and waste out the middle. Flip the piece end for end to cut the dado on the other side of the spacer. Repeat the process on the other face of the workpiece. Finally, raise the dado blade and cut the deeper dadoes into the top of the feet and the bottom of the cross rails (bottom left).

Tackle the posts and stretcher

To finish the bridle joints, the two-piece posts need to be notched on the top and bottom to accept the top cross rail and foot. I cut the notch with the post upright on the tablesaw in a jig that slides on the tablesaw fence. I cut the two cheeks, cut out the waste on the bandsaw, and then finish up the flat between the cheeks at the bench. I undercut the middle slightly to ensure a tight fit.

Next I cut the half laps connecting the posts to the lower stretcher. First I cut

Cut half laps on the stretcher. This piece is long and heavy, so Soto sets up a stop on a miter gauge and cuts the closest edge of the notch on one side, flips to the other face and cuts the opposite side, flips to the other end, and repeats. Then he resets the stop to cut the farthest edge of the notch and repeats. Finally, he wastes away the middle.

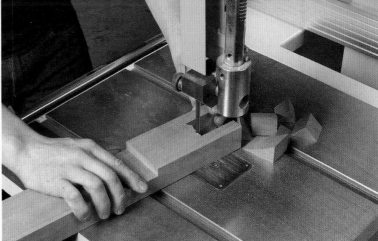

Tablesaw, bandsaw, chisel. Each post gets notched on the top and bottom to complete the bridle joint on the top cross rail and foot. With the post on end in a jig on the tablesaw (far left) cut the two cheeks. Then cut out the center waste on the bandsaw (above) and finish up the flat between the cheeks at the bench (left).

the stretcher to length. It's long, so I use a jig to keep the stock from tipping down. When laying out the joint, make sure you compensate for the ¼-in. spacer that will separate the two halves of the posts. I use a dado set to cut the joint.

Now use a ⅜-in.-dia. brad-point bit to drill holes for the pegs that go through the posts.

Time for dry-fitting and fine-tuning

Clean up and fit all the joints at the bench. After the joints are satisfactory, dry-fit all the parts. Then mark for the peg holes in the stretcher with the bit you used to drill the holes in the posts.

Next, lay out the half laps joining the top stretchers to the cross rails and cross supports. Cut 15° bevels on the ends of the cross rails, the cross supports, and top

Pegs are a design detail. Locate and drill holes in the posts (left). Dry-fit the feet, stretcher, and posts, and use a brad-point bit to mark the peg location in the stretcher (right). Disassemble and drill the stretcher.

Half-lap grid supports the top. Dry-assemble the base, mark the locations for all the half laps on the intersecting pieces, and cut them on the tablesaw.

stretchers. I use a chopsaw and then clean up the ends with a sanding block.

Now back to the feet. Use a template to mark the tapers on the top of each foot. I cut the angles on the bandsaw and clean up the bandsaw marks with a block plane and sanding block.

You'll want to relieve the bottoms of the feet so that there are fewer points of contact on the floor. I come in about 6 in. from each side and then stop in the middle where the post touches the floor. I relieve 3/16 in. from the bottom, making sure to score both sides of the foot to reduce tearout. I use stops on either end of the miter-gauge fence and hog out the waste with a dado set, making sure the blade comes up to the score line. I use a backer piece to reduce tearout even further.

Drill holes through the stretcher with the 3/8-in. brad point bit that was used to mark the location of the pegs. Then, drill and elongate the holes for the screws to attach the top.

Feet get tapered and relieved. Cut the taper with a bandsaw and clean up the surfaces with a plane and sanding block. Then relieve the bottoms with a dado blade and two stops on the tablesaw.

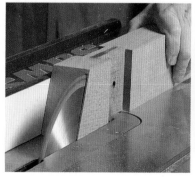

Angle and thin the end of the stretchers. After cutting the angle on each end of the stretcher on the miter saw, use the tablesaw to trim the block beyond the half lap. With the blade fully raised, rip in and back out (left). Snap off the thin waste (right) and clean up with a block plane.

Sand and glue it up

Before assembly, I finish-sand and apply finish to the inside surfaces between the posts and to the spacers themselves, being careful to avoid getting finish on any of the joinery. For the glue-up, I like to use a slower-setting glue to allow myself a little more time and a lot less stress. Titebond III is good for this.

It can be a little tricky getting all the parts together at once, so a dry run is a good idea. I do not glue in the top stretchers and the cross supports. I like to leave these dry for transportation and any tricky doorways or tight corners that may have to be worked around during a delivery. I do dry-fit them during glue-up to help keep things aligned.

Last, add the four pegs that come in halfway through the leg on each side, protruding slightly. I make my own and prefinish them. I ebonize the ends that will protrude and mask off the ends that will be glued in.

Prefinish the inside of the posts. Because the space between the posts is so narrow, you must finish the inside of the posts and the spacers between them before assembly.

Stretcher, posts, and feet. The first step of the glue-up is to sandwich the stretcher in between the posts and add the two feet.

Add the top cross rails. Glue and tap the cross rails into place (left). Dry-fit the top stretchers (right) and the cross supports. These pieces help keep things aligned during glue-up, but are left dry so the table can be disassembled for transportation and maneuvering through tricky doorways or tight corners.

Pair a subtle natural edge with the angular base. Soto prefers a full spline (above) over Dominoes or biscuits because it's easier to align the pieces in the glue-up with a full spline. Because Soto chose boards without too much wave, he doesn't have to use shaped cauls when clamping (right). He does put shims into any cracks that will get butterfly keys so the clamping pressure doesn't affect them. Screw the top to the base through elongated holes in the cross supports underneath (bottom right).

Top it off

For this tabletop, I used book-matched planks of black walnut that are about 18 in. wide. I made a router jig to flatten the top and edge-glued the two pieces together. Generally, with tabletops I like to add a spline between the two pieces for alignment and reinforcement. Alternatively, you can use Dominoes or biscuits. I also used a spring joint for the edges.

Finally, I used Osmo Polyx-Oil for the finish. I used four coats on the top and two on the base. When working with walnut, I wet-sand the first coat to fill in the grain. I find this helps with spills and overall durability.

Metric Equivalents

INCHES	CENTIMETERS	MILLIMETERS	INCHES	CENTIMETERS	MILLIMETERS
⅛	0.3	3	13	33.0	330
¼	0.6	6	14	35.6	356
⅜	1.0	10	15	38.1	381
½	1.3	13	16	40.6	406
⅝	1.6	16	17	43.2	432
¾	1.9	19	18	45.7	457
⅞	2.2	22	19	48.3	483
1	2.5	25	20	50.8	508
1¼	3.2	32	21	53.3	533
1½	3.8	38	22	55.9	559
1¾	4.4	44	23	58.4	584
2	5.1	51	24	61	610
2½	6.4	64	25	63.5	635
3	7.6	76	26	66.0	660
3½	8.9	89	27	68.6	686
4	10.2	102	28	71.7	717
4½	11.4	114	29	73.7	737
5	12.7	127	30	76.2	762
6	15.2	152	31	78.7	787
7	17.8	178	32	81.3	813
8	20.3	203	33	83.8	838
9	22.9	229	34	86.4	864
10	25.4	254	35	88.9	889
11	27.9	279	36	91.4	914
12	30.5	305			

Contributors

Todd Bradlee, who began using power tools at age 12, is a professional furniture maker in Bishop, Calif.

Anatole Burkin is an author and woodworker who lives in Santa Rosa, Calif. He is the former editor and publisher of *Fine Woodworking*.

Timothy Coleman is a professional furniture maker in Shelburne, Mass.

Michael Cullen makes custom furniture, sculpture, boxes, and frames in Petaluma, Calif.

Kelly J. Dunton of Terryville, Conn., has a meticulous eye for all things mechanical.

Mark Edmundson is a professional furniture and cabinet maker in Sandpoint, Idaho.

Jerry C. Forshee is a furniture maker in Bloomington, Ind.

Michael Fortune is a *Fine Woodworking* contributing editor.

Duncan Gowdy works in his one-man shop in Holden, Mass.

Reed Hansuld makes custom furniture in Brooklyn, N.Y.

Roland Johnson is a *Fine Woodworking* contributing editor. He wrote the book on bandsaws *(Taunton's Complete Illustrated Guide to Bandsaws*, The Taunton Press, 2010).

Ellen Kaspern, a professional woodworker in Boston, teaches at North Bennet Street School.

Mike Korsak makes custom furniture in Pittsburgh, Pa.

Steve Latta is a *Fine Woodworking* contributing editor and teaches woodworking at Thaddeus Stevens College of Technology in Lancaster, Pa.

Jeff Miller builds furniture in his storefront shop in Chicago, and teaches woodworking classes there and around the country. Go to furnituremaking.com for information.

William Peck, a retired engineer, was the *Fine Woodworking* shop manager.

Gary Rogowski is the director of The Northwest Woodworking Studio, a school for woodworkers in Portland, Ore.

Timothy Rousseau is a professional furniture maker who also teaches at the Center for Furniture Craftsmanship in Rockport, Maine.

Marcus Soto is design and production partner at New York Heartwoods in Kingston, N.Y. He also is the owner of Sojen Design, a custom furniture company located in the Hudson Valley.

Doug Stowe, based in Eureka Springs, Ark., is a box maker and woodworking instructor. His most recent book is *Tiny Boxes* (The Taunton Press, 2016).

Craig Thibodeau is a professional furniture maker in San Diego (ctfinefurniture.com) and author of *The Craft of Veneering* (The Taunton Press, 2018).

Bob Van Dyke is the founder and director of the Connecticut Valley School of Woodworking and teaches at other guilds and schools.

Credits

All photos are courtesy of *Fine Woodworking* magazine, © The Taunton Press, Inc., except as noted below.

Front Cover: Shutterstock

The articles in this book appeared in the following issues of *Fine Woodworking*:

pp. 5–11: Cabinet Saws for the Home Shop by Roland Johnson, issue 251. Photos by Kelly J. Dunton, except photo p. 5 and top two photos p. 6 by Matt Kenney, bottom left photo p. 6 by John Tetreault, and bottom right photo p. 6 and bottom photos p. 11 by Roland Johnson.

pp. 12–18: Tune Your Tablesaw by Ellen Kaspern, issue 265. Photos by Barry NM Dima. Drawings by Vince Babak.

pp. 19–25: Tablesaw Blades for Joinery by Bob Van Dyke, issue 253. Photos by Dillon Ryan. Drawings by Kelly J. Dunton.

pp. 26–31: Shopmade Tablesaw Inserts by Bob Van Dyke, issue 251. Photos by Dillon Ryan. Drawing by Michael Pekovich.

pp. 32–39: Essential Bandsaw Blades by Roland Johnson, issue 252. Photos by Dillon Ryan, except for top photo p. 33 by John Tetreault. Drawings by John Tetreault.

pp. 40–47: Tool Test: Drill Presses by William Peck, issue 249. Photos by Asa Christiana, except photos p. 42, p. 46, and p. 47 by John Tetreault.

pp. 48–52: Fundamentals: What drill bits do you really need? by Roland Johnson, issue 258. Photos by *Fine Woodworking* staff.

pp. 53–60: Tool Test: Benchtop Planers by Kelly J. Dunton, issue 253. Photos by Matt Kenney.

pp. 61–65: Tool Test: Track Saws by Mark Edmundson, issue 255. Action photos by Asa Christiana; product photos by Michael Pekovich.

pp. 66–74: Add Bushings to Your Router Kit by Jeff Miller, issue 263. Photos by Asa Christiana. Drawings by Dan Thornton.

pp. 75–82: Dust Collection for the Small Shop by Anatole Burkin, issue 258. Photos by Asa Christiana.

pp. 84–88: Fundamentals: The physics of machine safety by Todd Bradlee, issue 265. Photos by Matt Kenney. Drawings by John Tetreault.

pp. 89–96: Safe Ripping on the Tablesaw by Bob Van Dyke, issue 266. Photos by Barry NM Dima. Drawings by Dan Thornton.

pp. 97–104: 3 Handy Stop Blocks by Bob Van Dyke, issue 260. Photos by Matt Kenney. Drawings by John Tetreault.

pp. 105–112: Simple Box-Joint Sled by Doug Stowe, issue 267. Photos by Barry NM Dima. Drawings by Vince Babak.

pp. 113–120: Tablesaw Sled for Miters by Craig Thibodeau, issue 257. Photos by Thomas McKenna. Drawings by Vince Babak.

pp. 121–130: Add Muscle to Your Miters by Duncan Gowdy, Timothy Coleman, and Reed Hansul, issue 254. Photos by Jonathan Binzen, except bottom right photo p. 122 by Dean Powell, bottom right photo p. 125 by Timothy Coleman, and top right photo p. 128 and top photo p. 130 by Reed Hansuld.

pp. 131–135: Shoulder Your Dovetails by Steve Latta, issue 259. Photos by Anissa Kapsales. Drawing by Bob La Pointe.

pp. 136-142: Thick Tabletops from Thin Stock by Mark Edmundson, issue 261. Photos by Asa Christiana, except photo p. 136 by David Marx. Drawings by Kelly J. Dunton.

pp. 143–151: Learn to Resaw by Timothy Rousseau, issue 253. Photos by Matt Kenney. Drawings by Dan Thornton.

pp. 152–159: Get Better Cuts with Your Planer by Jerry C. Forshee, issue 256. Photos by Dillon Ryan. Drawings by Vince Babak.

pp. 160–167: Drill Press Tips and Tricks by Michael Fortune, issue 252. Photos by Asa Christiana. Drawings by Vince Babak.

pp. 168–175: Sanding on the Drill Press by Michael Fortune, issue 254. Photos by Asa Christiana. Drawings by Kelly J. Dunton.

pp. 176–180: Fundamentals: Get started with your plunge router by Jeff Miller, issue 256. Photos by Asa Christiana. Drawings by John Tetreault.

pp. 181–188: Easy Angled Tenons by Jeff Miller, issue 260. Photos by Asa Christiana. Drawings by Dan Thornton.

pp. 190–194: Build a Perfect Picture Frame by Michael Cullen, issue 264. Photos by Jonathan Binzen. Drawings by Dan Thornton.

pp. 195–204: Build a Collector's Case by Gary Rogowski, issue 249. Photos by Steve Scott, except bottom photo p. 195 by John Tetreault. Drawings by Christopher Mills.

pp. 205–212: Beautiful Bandsawn Boxes by Michael Cullen, issue 250. Photos by Jonathan Binzen, except photos p. 205 and p. 206 and box photos p. 210-212 by John Tetreault. Drawings by Christopher Mills.

pp. 213–222: Elegant Bookcase Top to Bottom by Mike Korsak, issue 264. Photos by Jonathan Binzen, except for photo p. 213 and top left photo p. 216 by Mike Korsak. Drawings by John Hartman.

pp. 223–231: A Fresh Take on the Trestle Table by Marcus Soto, issue 262. Photos by Anissa Kapsales. Drawings by Christopher Mills.

Index